DEPTH PSYCHOLOGY
AND A NEW ETHIC

A C. G. JUNG FOUNDATION BOOK
PUBLISHED IN ASSOCIATION WITH DAIMON VERLAG
EINSIEDELN, SWITZERLAND

The C. G. Jung Foundation for Analytical Psychology is dedicated to helping men and women grow in conscious awareness of the psychological realities in themselves and society, find healing and meaning in their lives and greater depth in their relationships, and live in response to their discovered sense of purpose. It welcomes the public to attend its lectures, seminars, films, symposia, and workshops and offers a wide selection of books for sale through its bookstore. The Foundation also publishes *Quadrant*, a semiannual journal, and books on Analytical Psychology and related subjects. For information about Foundation programs or membership, please write to the C. G. Jung Foundation, 28 East 39th Street, New York, NY 10016.

DEPTH PSYCHOLOGY AND A NEW ETHIC

Erich Neumann

Translated by
EUGENE ROLFE

Forewords by
C. G. Jung, Gerhard Adler & James Yandell

SHAMBHALA
Boston & London
1990

SHAMBHALA PUBLICATIONS, INC.
Horticultural Hall
300 Massachusetts Avenue
Boston, Massachusetts 02115
www.shambhala.com

First Shambhala Edition
Printed in the United States of America on acid-free paper
Distributed in the United States by Random House
and in Canada by Random House of Canada Ltd.
Distributed in the United Kingdom by Element Books Ltd.

LIBRARY OF CONGRESS CATALOGING-IN-PUBLICATION DATA
Neumann, Erich.
    [Tiefenpsychologie und neue Ethik. English]
    Depth psychology and a new ethic / Erich Neumann: translated by Eugene Rolfe.
        p.   cm.
    Translation of: Tiefenpsychologie und neue Ethik.
    Reprint. Originally published: New York: Putnam's, 1969.
    "Published in association with Daimon Verlag Einsiedeln."
    "A C. G. Jung Foundation book."
    ISBN 0-87773-571-9 (alk. paper)
    1. Shadow (Psychoanalysis) 2. Good and evil—Psychological aspects. 3. Ethics—Psychological aspects. 4. Psychoanalysis.
    I. Title.
BF175.5.S55N48   1990   89-29554
150.19'54—dc20   CIP
BVG 01

CONTENTS

FOREWORD

by James Yandell

We are all born with much the same human nature. That nature includes, in potential form, capacities for such virtues as loving generosity, compassion, altruism, courage, patience, and wisdom. It also includes potentials for other qualities like callous selfishness, greed, envy, cowardice, cruelty, pettiness, destructive violence, and willful unconsciousness.

Before we have been long in the world, we begin to learn that some aspects of our nature and expression win approval from the powerful giants on whom we are dependent, but that other elements are not so acceptable. Needing the love of others and our own self-esteem, we cultivate in ourselves whatever is rewarded as "good" and try to exclude from our behavior and sense of self that which is disapproved and punished as "bad." The contents of this distinction vary, but the process of socializing and shaping a child by the reinforcement of approval and disapproval, reward and punishment, is universal.

The environment's response to us during our early years in the family is the foundation of our sense of good and bad in ourselves. It is followed in later years by the inculcation of our society's values by school, church, mass media, and other social institutions. The psyche tends to formulate experience in terms of paired opposites. In our culture socialization intensifies this predisposition; we are taught to distinguish, separate, and split—especially to split good versus bad. We are taught to aspire to goodness, even perfection, to identify with the "positive" side of our nature, while denying and disowning the "negative." The resulting split state is considered normal.

Our identification with the good gives us a permanent bad conscience and sense of fraudulence, for at some level we know we are not what we aspire to and pretend to be. What becomes of the rejected portion of our humanness? How do we deal with what C. G. Jung called "the part of us that we don't want to be part of us"? In general, we try to repress it from consciousness and exclude it from our self-definition as we identify with the light. But it is no less real for being banished from ego territory. Quite the contrary: removed from conscious awareness and control, it gains autonomous power. It is full of energy and has ways of finding expression, often in forms clearly visible to others, if not to us.

This disowned portion of our nature is part of what Jung named the "shadow." The optical metaphor recognizes that shadow is produced by light and is the shadow *of* the light, the consequence and inverse of consciousness. The shadow includes primitive and undeveloped portions that have never been conscious, as well as that which has been experienced and rejected by the ego; at times Jung equated the shadow with the whole unconscious. It has individual and personal levels; what I edit out of my self-concept and official identity will differ somewhat from what you exclude from yours. There is a cultural level; one nation's notions of good and evil are different from another's. And there are collective, universal levels of shadow, such as our uniquely human aggression and destructiveness, which threaten to destroy the planet by nuclear war, pollution, and reckless consumption.

Simple repression is not sufficient to sustain one's sense of virtue and superiority. It is necessary that the excluded shadow contents go somewhere, have outer form, be personified. For Dr. Jekyll to be stable as Dr. Jekyll, Mr. Hyde is required. Projection is added to repression, and the rejected

2

elements of the personality find a repository "out there." Whatever is denied and disowned at home is discovered in another person or group and there seen as inferior and subhuman, the villain and enemy. This is a much more satisfactory arrangement. One can now feel comfortably free of taint as one despises, condemns, and attacks one's projected evil in others. This can occur in the individual or at the group level. Or one state may denounce another as "the evil empire" or "the great Satan." Individual or collective self-esteem is supported by prosecuting the struggle against the enemy, often with the expressed aim of destroying him and eradicating evil forever in a final triumph of light over darkness. Hitler's projection of evil onto the Jews logically led to his program of purifying Germany by exterminating them. In wanting to make Germany *Judenrein*, Hitler was one of the world's great idealists, which should leave us with a permanent lesson about purity and idealism.

A further step in this process is *mutual* shadow projection, in which each of a pair of persons, groups, or states serves as the perceived enemy of the other. These arrangements can be remarkably stable and long-lasting. The adversarial dance between polarized opponents may be contained and ritualized, as in the duel of some marriages, formal debate, two-party politics, bipolar sports, and other zero-sum games in which one side wins to the extent that the other loses. Or it may be uncontrolled and immensely dangerous, as in race conflict or in "cold war" between adversary pairs of states whose stability rests precariously on the deterrent threat of "mutual assured destruction." In an age of nuclear armaments trigger-ready for overkill, mutual shadow projection becomes an unaffordable and potentially catastrophic indulgence. With the apparent end of the cold war, there has been some recognition in American thought of the problem of our loss of a clear and pure enemy. The economic success of the Japanese may fill this need with a resurgence of the

Yellow Peril to replace the Red Menace.

Critical judgment is not necessarily shadow projection. But when the finger is pointed, it is useful to look not only at where it points, but also back at the finger-pointer to see what motivation and benefit might reside there. Self-elevation by denouncing others is so tempting and gratifying, and so universal, that no condemnation of apparent evil should be taken entirely at face value.

Psychologically, the only effective alternative to shadow projection with its attendant hazards and costs is its opposite: shadow recognition, acknowledgment, and integration. This is the subject of Erich Neumann's precious volume, made again available in this new edition. What Neumann calls the "old ethic"—the Western religious and psychological tradition that sets spiritual perfection as its standard and goal—requires that we own only the "good" part of our nature and sustain this inflated self-idealization by projecting the negative onto others. The insights of depth psychology, he believes, offer us permission and means to move beyond this practice to a "new ethic" in which, freed from the futile ambition and requirement of perfection, we can own and deal with all of our nature. In this orientation the highest value is no longer perfection, but wholeness and reality. Such an ethic requires that we recognize and deal directly with our unwelcome humanness rather than project it onto an enemy who, as carrier of our rejected shadow, becomes a psychological necessity for us even while we seek to destroy him.

Neumann's proposal is revolutionary. As every psychotherapist knows, the withdrawal of projections is the most central and difficult part of the work. Finding and hating one's own "evil" in others is familiar and habitual, and paradoxically comfortable even when one is in a paranoid rage. Giving up the benefits of such projection is arduous, slow, and uncertain. One's self-esteem is at least temporarily damaged, as one's scrutiny turns from the mote in the other's eye to the beam in one's own. Perhaps even more difficult than acknowledging our wickedness, which at least has a certain glamour, is recognizing our ordinariness; the banality of our foundation as mortal animals can be painfully deflating. But there is gold in the muck, and as shadow integration proceeds, one reclaims substance, energy, and creative imagination that have been consigned to the sewer or to the devil. One has the strength that comes from being in accord with reality rather than in desperate defense of a false self-idealization, and one recognizes the high cost and true poverty of the previous identification with the good. The ultimate net effect of the shift from the old ethic to the new is relief, revitalization, and a new competence to deal with real rather than invented problems. One moves toward wholeness.

If this is difficult for motivated and psychologically minded persons in the safety of the analytic container, what can we hope for at the collective level? Neumann's vision may be wishful fantasy. Yet daily we analysts see in our practices that such changes do occur in individuals as part of their therapeutic work and individuation. In collective life, shared experience and awareness of danger, like the threat of atmospheric destruction or nuclear annihilation, can produce new consciousness of a common enemy, transcending the prior adversarial structure. Ecology, with its recognition of the wholeness of the earth and its vulnerable interdependence of parts and processes, is almost entirely a development of the past few decades, a product of our being forced to recognize the *self*-destructiveness of our abuse of the environment. A political ecology is also developing; national boundaries are increasingly artificial, and "one world" has progressed from wished-for ideal to commonly experienced fact. Neumann in effect proposes a psychological ecology in which all parts of the psychic system are to be recognized, owned, and integrated into a whole functioning. This may also be possible. It surely is necessary.

Jung said in 1959, in response to interviewer John Freeman's question about the likelihood of world war, "We are so full of apprehensions, fears, that one doesn't know exactly to what it points. One thing is sure. A great change of our psychological attitude is imminent. That is certain." Part of such a great change may be the vision elaborated by Neumann in this volume: "The time has now come for the principle of perfection to be sacrificed on the altar of wholeness."

Depth Psychology and a New Ethic has had a difficult history. Around the time of its publication in 1949, there was considerable opposition among Jung's Zurich followers to Neumann and to the book, and it was rejected for inclusion in the official list of Jungian publications. This may have had to do with the thorny problem of the relation between individual inner moral authority and outer collective authority as raised in Neumann's "new ethic." Or it may have represented reaction to Neumann's assertive style, jealousy among Jung's disciples toward the intruder from Tel Aviv whom Jung regarded so highly, or Jungian anti-Semitism. Despite Jung's endorsement and foreword, the book did not appear in English for another twenty years. While Neumann's other works have become Jungian classics, this book has been relatively neglected and in recent years has been out of print in English. In its richness, succinctness, and urgent relevance to our times it may ultimately prove to be his most valuable work, and its renewed availability is cause for rejoicing.

In the 1959 interview Jung went on to say, "We need more understanding of human nature, because the only real danger that exists is man himself. . . . We know nothing of man, far too little. His psyche should be studied, because we are the origin of all coming evil." In this volume Neumann has made a major contribution to that study.

James Yandell
San Francisco

1990

6

FOREWORD TO THIS EDITION

by Dr. Gerhard Adler

When Dr. Neumann's *Depth Psychology and a New Ethic* was first published in German, in 1949, it aroused considerable controversy. It was perhaps unfortunate that it was the first of his books to appear, since it thus lacked the solid basis of thought and evidence which his great book on *The Origins and History of Consciousness* — published a few months after the *New Ethic* — could have given to his approach to the problem of ethics.

No such difficulty arises with the English translation. Dr. Neumann's work is by now well represented in English translations: apart from the *Origins*, published in 1954, there is the classic monograph on *The Great Mother* (1955), his commentary on *Amor and Psyche* (1956), *Art and the Creative Unconscious* (1959), and *The Archetypal World of Henry Moore* (1959). With these publications Neumann's work — by many considered to be the most original and outstanding contribution to Jung's thought — and his place in Analytical Psychology are firmly established.

Among all his books the *New Ethic* has a special place. It is a passionate appeal to the conscience and consciousness of our time, a deeply personal statement of faith in the future of modern man, a future based on an ever-growing awareness of his psychological problems and their solutions.

To Neumann the basic problem of modern man is the problem of evil: conventional ethics have proved incapable of

7

containing or transforming its destructive forces. But the "dark" side has invaded the world image of modern man with a vengeance, and no longer is he certain of his position regarding good and evil.

Thus what modern man needs most is an awareness of evil, and first of all of evil within himself: of his own "dark" inferior personality, his own shadow. This side has only too often and too easily been seen in, "projected" into, the other person – one way of satisfying the well-known need to find a scapegoat for one's own shortcomings. As a result we have split the world into "good" and "bad", superior and inferior nations, races, or individuals, with catastrophic consequences.

Awareness of evil challenges the individual: he has to learn to realise, acknowledge, and live with his own dark side. Instead of suppressing, or repressing, the shadow and consequently projecting it outside, it has to be integrated. Only thus can modern man achieve fuller consciousness and a higher degree of integration; the ambiguity of one's own existence, the awareness of both positive and negative forces within the individual and the collective becomes the point of departure for a new ethical attitude. In Neumann's words: "Acceptance of the shadow is the essential basis for the actual achievement of an ethical attitude towards the 'Thou' who is outside me."

But this can lead to a conflict with collective values: the decisive ethical authority no longer rests with collective values of good and evil and with a conventional "conscience" but with an inner "Voice" – a constant challenge to individual decision and responsibility, even where it may lead to a rejection of collective morality.

It is a radical ethic, based on the most stringent demand for individual choice and courage. It involves a continuous confrontation of man with the problem of good and evil arising from the honest acceptance of human totality – the totality of the individual and the totality of mankind. To quote Neumann once more: "The individual must work through his own basic moral problem before he is in a position to play a responsible part in the collective."

On account of its radical demand for individual choice and for obedience to the inner voice, Neumann's position has sometimes been grossly misunderstood.[1] One well-meaning critic even thought that in that case every madman who heard voices could set himself up as an ethical genius. This is the precise opposite to Neumann's real concern, which is the most exacting and profoundly moral requirement for everlasting self-questioning and constant wakefulness regarding one's motives. If anything, Neumann's ethical demands make the individual burden almost too heavy to bear; but then his challenge is one to man in the continuous process of development and has to be understood as a signpost pointing into the future.

I would like to conclude with a few sentences from a letter which C. G. Jung wrote to Neumann in December 1948 when the first reactions to the *New Ethic* had made themselves felt:[2] ". . . I have read your book once more. Again it made a very strong impression on me and with that gave me the certainty that its effect would be like a bomb. Your formulations are brilliant and of piercing precision; they are challenging and aggressive, an *avant-garde* in open country where, alas, nothing was visible before. Naturally the enemy concentrates his fire on this uncovered troop. It is just the convincingly clear, because unequivocal, formula which has an exposed flank. No war is ever conducted without losses, and a static balance leads nowhere. Already the title *New Ethic* is a fanfare: '*aux armes, citoyens!*' . . . Your book will be a *petra scandali*, but also the most

[1] Dr. Neumann was concerned about this misunderstanding, and for this reason wrote a special preface to the Spanish edition in 1959, which has also been included in this translation.

[2] Jung and several of the author's colleagues saw the manuscript before publication.

powerful impulse for future developments. For this I am profoundly grateful to you . . ."

I hope that Neumann's book will be read and understood in the spirit expressed in Jung's letter.

Gerhard Adler

1968

FOREWORD

by Professor C. G. Jung[1]

translated by R. F. C. Hull

The author has asked me if I would write a foreword to the present book. I am happy to comply with this request, although it is only as an empiricist, and never as a philosopher, that I have been concerned with depth psychology, and cannot boast of ever having tried my hand at formulating ethical principles. My professional work has certainly given me plenty of opportunities to do this, since the chief causes of a neurosis are conflicts of conscience and difficult moral problems that require an answer. The psychotherapist thus finds himself in an extremely awkward situation. Having learnt by long and often painful experience the relative ineffectiveness of trying to inculcate moral precepts, he has to abandon all admonitions and exhortations that begin with "ought" and "must". In addition, with increasing experience and knowledge of psychic relationships, the conviction dwindles away that he knows exactly what is good and bad in every individual case. His *vis-à-vis*, the other person, is indeed "another", a profound stranger, if ever the discussion should penetrate to the core of the problem, namely the unique individuality of the patient. What is then meant by "good"? Good for him? Good for me? Good for his relatives? Good for society? Our judgement becomes so hopelessly caught in a tangle of subsidiary considerations and

[1] This Foreword was written by Jung in 1949 for an English edition of the book which did not then materialise.

relationships that, unless circumstances compel us to cut through the Gordian knot, we would do better to leave it alone, or content ourselves with offering the sufferer what modest help we can in unravelling the threads.

For these reasons it is particularly difficult for the medical psychologist to formulate any ethical principles. I do not mean that such a task does not exist, or that its solution is absolutely impossible. I fully recognise that there is an urgent need today to formulate the ethical problem anew, for, as the author aptly points out, an entirely new situation has arisen since modern psychology broadened its scope by the study of unconscious processes. Concurrently with this, things have happened in Europe, and still go on happening, that far surpass the horrors of imperial Rome or the French reign of terror; things that have ruthlessly revealed the weakness of our whole system of ethics.

Moral principles that seem clear and unequivocal from the standpoint of ego-consciousness lose their power of conviction, and hence their applicability, when we consider the *compensatory significance of the shadow* in the light of ethical responsibility. No man endowed with any ethical sense can avoid doing this. Only a man who is repressed or morally stupid will be able to neglect this task, though he will not be able to get rid of the evil consequences of such behaviour. (In this respect the author utters some heartening truths.)

The tremendous revolution of values that has been brought about by the discovery of the unconscious, with repercussions still to come, is scarcely understood today or even noticed. The psychological foundation of all philosophical assertions, for example, is still assiduously overlooked or deliberately obscured, so much so that certain modern philosophies unconsciously lay themselves open to psychological attack. The same is true of ethics.

It is, understandably enough, the medical psychologist who is the first to be impressed by the shortcomings or evils of the epoch, for he is the first to have to deal with its casualties. The treatment of neurosis is not, in the last resort, a technical problem, but a moral one. There are, admittedly, interim solutions that are technical, but they never result in the kind of ethical attitude that could be described as a real cure. Although every act of conscious realisation is at least a step forward on the road to individuation, to the "making whole" of the individual, the integration of the personality is unthinkable without the responsible, and that means moral, relation of the parts to one another, just as the constitution of a state is impossible without mutual relations between its members. The ethical problem thus poses itself, and it is primarily the task of the psychologist to provide an answer or to help his patient find one. Often this work is wearisome and difficult, because it cannot be accomplished by intellectual short cuts or moral recipes, but only by careful observation of the inner and outer conditions. Patience and time are needed for the gradual crystallisation of a goal and a direction for which the patient can take responsibility. The analyst learns that ethical problems are always intensely individual, and can convince himself again and again that the collective rules of conduct offer at most provisional solutions, but never lead to those crucial decisions which are the turning-points in a man's life. As the author rightly says: "The diversity and complexity of the situation make it impossible for us to lay down any theoretical rule of ethical behaviour."

The formulation of ethical rules is not only difficult but actually impossible because one can hardly think of a single rule that would not have to be reversed under certain conditions. Even the simple proposition "Conscious realisation is good" is only of limited validity, since we not infrequently meet with situations in which conscious realisation would have the worst possible consequences. I have therefore made it a rule to take the "old ethic" as binding only so long as there is no evidence of its injurious effects. But if dangerous consequences threaten, one is then faced with a problem of the first order,[1] the solution of which challenges the personality to the limit and demands the maximum of attention, patience and time. The solution, in my experience, is always individual and is only subjectively valid. In such a situation, all those reflections which the author passes under review have to be considered very seriously. Despite their subjective nature, they cannot very well be formulated except as collective concepts. But since these reflections constantly recur in practice — for the integration of unconscious contents continually poses such questions — it necessarily follows that, in spite of individual variation, they will exhibit certain regular features which make it seem possible to abstract a limited number of rules. I do not, myself, think that any of these rules are absolutely valid, for on occasion the opposite may be equally true. That is what makes the integration of the unconscious so difficult: we have to learn to think in antinomies, constantly bearing in mind that every truth turns into an antinomy if it is thought out to the end. All our statements about the unconscious are "eschatological" truths, that is, borderline concepts which formulate a partially apprehended fact or situation, and are therefore only conditionally valid.

The ethical problems that cannot be solved in the light of collective morality or the "old ethic" are *conflicts of duty*, otherwise they would not be ethical. Although I do not share Friedrich Theodor Vischer's optimistic view that morality is always self-evident, I am nevertheless of the opinion that in working out a difficult problem the moral aspect of it has to be considered if one is to avoid a repression or a deception. He who deceives others deceives himself, and vice versa. Nothing is gained by that, least of all the integration of the shadow. Indeed, its integration makes the highest demands on an individual's morality, for the "acceptance of evil" means nothing less than

[1] "The most wretched of inventors are those who invent a new morality: they are always immoralists," says a French aphorist.

that his whole moral existence is put in question. Decisions of the most momentous kind are called for. The alchemical dictum "The art requires the whole man" is particularly true of the integration of the unconscious, and this process was in fact symbolically anticipated by the alchemists. It is evident, therefore, that the solution will be satisfactory only if it expresses the whole of the psyche. This is not possible unless the conscious mind takes account of the unconscious, unless desire is confronted with its possible consequences, and unless action is subjected to moral criticism.

Nor should it be forgotten that moral law is not just something imposed upon man from outside (for instance, by a crabbed grandfather). On the contrary, it expresses a psychic fact. As the regulator of action, it corresponds to a preformed image, a pattern of behaviour which is archetypal and deeply embedded in human nature. This has no fixed content; it represents the specific form which any number of different contents may take. For one person it is "good" to kill those who think differently from him; for another the supreme law is tolerance; for a third it is a sin to skin an animal with an iron knife; for a fourth it is disrespectful to step on the shadow of a chief. Fundamental to all these rules is "religious observation" or "careful consideration", and this involves a moral effort which is indispensable for the development of consciousness. A saying of Jesus in the *Codex Bezae* (referring to Luke 6:4) expresses it in lapidary form: "Man, if thou knowest what thou doest, thou art blessed. But if thou knowest not, thou art accursed and a transgressor of the law."

We might therefore define the "new ethic" as a development and differentiation within the old ethic, confined at present to those uncommon individuals who, driven by unavoidable conflicts of duty, endeavour to bring the conscious and the unconscious into responsible relationship.

In so far as ethics represent a system of moral demands, it follows that any innovations within or outside this system would also possess a "deontological" character. But the psychic situation to which the new admonition "you ought" would be applicable is so complicated, delicate and difficult that one wonders who would be in a position to make such a demand. Nor would it be needed at all since the ethically minded person who gets into a situation of this sort has already been confronted with this same demand, from within, and knows only too well that there is no collective morality that could extricate him from his dilemma. If the values of the old ethic were not seated in the very marrow of his bones, he would never have got into this situation in the first place. Let us take as an example the universally valid commandment: Thou shalt not lie. What is one to do if, as frequently happens to a doctor, one finds oneself in a situation where it would be a catastrophe to tell the truth or to suppress it? If one does not want to precipitate the catastrophe directly, one cannot avoid telling a convincing lie, prompted by psychological common sense, readiness to help, Christian charity, consideration for the fate of the other people concerned — in short, by ethical motives just as strong if not stronger than those which compel one to tell the truth. One comforts oneself with the excuse that it was done in a good cause and was therefore moral. But anyone who has insight will know that on the one hand he was too cowardly to precipitate a catastrophe, and on the other hand that he has lied shamelessly. He has done evil but at the same time good. No-one stands beyond good and evil, otherwise he would be out of this world. Life is a continual balancing of opposites, like every other energic process. The abolition of opposites would be equivalent to death. Neitzsche escaped the collision of opposites by going into the madhouse. The yogi attains the state of *nirdvandva* (freedom from opposites) in the rigid lotus position of non-conscious, non-acting *samadhi*. But the ordinary man stands between the opposites and knows that he can never abolish them. There is no good without evil, and no evil without good. The one conditions the other, but it does not become the other or abolish the other. If a man is endowed with an ethical sense and is convinced of the sanctity of ethical values, he is on the surest road to a conflict of duty. And although this looks desperately like a moral catastrophe, it alone makes possible a higher differentiation of ethics and a broadening of consciousness. A conflict of duty forces us to examine our conscience and thereby to discover the shadow. This, in turn, forces us to come to terms with the unconscious. The ethical aspect of this process of integration is described with praiseworthy clarity by the author.

Those who are unfamiliar with the psychology of the unconscious will have some difficulty in envisaging the role which the unconscious plays in the analytical process. The unconscious is a living psychic entity which, it seems, is relatively autonomous, behaving as if it were a personality with intentions of its own. At any rate it would be quite wrong to think of the unconscious as mere "material", or as a passive object to be used or exploited. Equally, its biological function is not just a mechanical one, in the sense that it is merely *complementary* to consciousness. It has far more the character of *compensation*, that is, an intelligent choice of means aiming not only at the restoration of the psychic equilibrium but at an advance towards wholeness. The reaction of the unconscious is far from being merely passive; it takes the initiative in a creative way, and sometimes its purposive activity predominates over its customary reactivity. As a partner in the process of conscious differentiation, it does not act as a mere opponent, for the revelation of its contents enriches consciousness and assists differentiation. A hostile opposition takes place only when consciousness obstinately clings to its one-sidedness and insists on its arbitrary standpoint, as always happens when there is a repression and, in consequence, a partial dissociation of consciousness.

Such being the behaviour of the unconscious, the process of coming to terms with it, in the ethical sense, acquires a special character. The process does not consist in dealing with a given "material", but in negotiating with a psychic minority (or majority, as the case may be) that has equal rights. For this reason the author compares the relation to the unconscious with a parliamentary democracy, whereas the old ethic unconsciously imitates, or actually prefers, the procedure of an absolute monarchy or a tyrannical one-party system. Through the new ethic, the ego-consciousness is ousted from its central position in a psyche organised on the lines of a monarchy or totalitarian state, its place being taken by *wholeness* or the *self*, which is now recognised as central. The self was of course always at the centre, and always acted as the hidden director. Gnosticism long ago projected this state of affairs into the heavens, in the form of a metaphysical drama: ego-consciousness appearing as the vain demiurge, who fancies himself the sole creator of the world, and the self as the highest, unknowable God, whose emanation the demiurge is. The union of conscious and unconscious in the individuation process, the real core of the ethical problem, was projected in the form of a drama of redemption and, in some Gnostic systems, consisted in the demiurge's discovery and recognition of the highest God.

This parallel may serve to indicate the magnitude of the problem we are concerned with, and to throw into relief the special character of the confrontation with the unconscious on an ethical plane. The problem is indeed a vital one. This may explain why the question of a new ethic is of such serious and urgent concern to the author, who argues his case with a boldness and passion well matched by his penetrating insight and thoughtfulness. I welcome this book as the first notable attempt to formulate the ethical problems raised by the discovery of the unconscious and to make them a subject for discussion.

C. G. Jung

March 1949

AUTHOR'S PREFACE

This book, which was conceived during the Second World War and under its direct impact, appears at a time that is already darkened by the louring spectre of a third world war. Have problems of ethics or even of a "new" ethic any relevance at all in an age dominated by a dance of death, to which National Socialism in Germany was little more than a prelude?

The nations which only yesterday were proclaiming their solidarity in the battle for the freedom of mankind, are now competing against each other in the production of atomic bombs; and who can doubt that the unthinkable of today will be the commonplace of tomorrow? What is the point, in a world situation such as this, of the ridiculous "ethical" question and the still more ridiculous answer, "It all depends on the individual"?

It may well appear that both question and answer are obsolete, and that all that is attempted in these pages is to meet the needs of a handful of individuals on the road to extinction. And yet everything combines to refute this contention. A historical consciousness which is able to survey the development of mankind as a whole is bound to recognise that the highest endeavour of the human species has always been devoted to the creation of the individual. The Community of Free Individuals is the next goal of evolution—still remote, but already visible on the horizon. However, community and freedom are not best proclaimed by atom bombs; nor can freedom and individuality be established by the monolithic state.

The shadow side of the human race towers over us all,

darkening the sky with its death-rays and its atom bombers. Yet the little creature, though always almost annihilated by the big battalions, always manages to survive, and David always triumphs over Goliath. It is the little creature that is the bearer of the divine miracle, for this little creature is nothing less than the creative individual, and it is under his guidance that the human race makes progress on its journey through history.

And so, in the last analysis, the little creature is in fact the greatest of all creatures; and it is only on the surface that a psychology which, at this time of all times, regards individuality as the central problem of community, appears to be fighting a losing battle. Again and again, these losing battles turn out to be the growing-points at which decisive developments take place for mankind.

Tel Aviv, Israel, May 1948   Erich Neumann

PREFACE TO THE SPANISH EDITION, 1959

My pleasure that this book is now to be translated into Spanish has been tempered by a certain anxiety. I have been obliged to face the question, "To what extent have I myself been responsible for the many misunderstandings which have come to light during the discussion of this book?" By this I mean neither protests on grounds of principle or ideology nor the objections (by no means rare!) made by critics who have not taken the trouble to give the book a careful reading. The need I feel to bring my reflections on the problem of a new ethic before the notice of the public seems to me no less compelling today than at the time when I originally wrote them. And yet the many occasions on which this need has been confirmed by readers to whom the book has given a helping hand in the task of clarifying their most important problems cannot in any way mitigate this anxiety.

One of the main lines of argument in this little book has been the attempt to establish the necessity for a hierarchical ethic — that is, to show that for men with different types of psychological make-up, different types of ethic are appropriate. At the same time, I have repeatedly stressed that the new ethic, with its changed attitude to evil, presupposes a man who is "moral" by the standards of the old ethic. The demands of the new ethic — if it is possible to speak of demands at all in this context — are higher and more exacting than those of the old. There is absolutely no question here of our being permitted to take things more easily than we were before. But modern man's experience of men and the world has increased; he has learned that it is no longer possible to capture life, with all its complexity and fateful power, in a single, simple moral formula such as "Thou shait do this" and "Thou shalt not do that"; and the truth is that he is now confronted with a compelling need for a new ethical orientation. It is precisely because the old religious and ethical values have lost their grip on modern man, and because he in turn has lost the grip on life which they used to give him, that he finds himself in a position of the gravest danger — a danger which only appears in a more obvious form in the sick people whom the psychotherapist meets in his consulting-room every day, but which equally affects those so-called normal persons who wage our wars, conduct our recurrent persecutions, and plan and prepare the necessary means for carrying these purposes into effect.

One expression of this grave moral crisis is the nihilistic despair about man which is an essential characteristic of the art and philosophy of our period. But the creative capacity of man and (though this is really the same thing) the creative capacity of the human psyche is deliberately overlooked in this context. On the other hand, depth psychology is essentially concerned with this very subject, and the creative quality in man and the methods of encouraging its authentic expression are in fact the basic problem of all psychotherapy.[1] The phenomena with

[1] See the author's paper on "Das Schöpferische als Zentralproblem der

which this book deals and on which it bases its conclusions are none other than these same creative processes which, with their tendency towards the goal of wholeness, are to be found at work in modern man.

The main cause of the difficulty which has been experienced in understanding what this book is about, and the source of most of the misunderstandings which it has encountered, is to be found in the present widespread ignorance as to what is happening psychologically within modern man. The ethical problem is, in fact, only a part of the general problem of the inner transformation now taking place in modern man; and to explain more clearly how — and why — this is so, I have added to the book in the form of an Appendix my "Reflections on the Shadow",[1] in which, perhaps, this complex of relationships receives a more explicit emphasis and also — more important still — is given its proper position and status in the whole range of problems which beset us.

Some attempt to indicate the way which modern man is being compelled to travel in his confrontation with evil — and this, neither more nor less, is our subject — should certainly be regarded as an urgent priority, since consciously or unconsciously the problem of evil is burning inside the heart of each one of us. Such a sense of urgency did — as I gladly admit, at this interval of time — give a sharper edge to some of my formulations — without however, in my view, making them too sharp. I have not been able to bring myself to alter these formulations, as has been suggested to me. The belligerent tone of much of this book is attributable, not only to the temperament of its author, but also to the fact that it amounts to a declaration of war against an ethic whose practical impotence has brought modern man to the brink of despair. It gives me no pleasure to be "a source of annoyance"; it is, however, precisely the deep and, as I see

[1] From *Der Psychologe*, Vol. II, No. 7/8, 1950.

Psychotherapie" at the Fourth International Congress for Medical Psychotherapy, Barcelona, 1950.

it, religious responsibility which weighs so heavily on the psycho-therapist today that forbids him to be vague, especially in a situation in which it is often the very wishy-washy vagueness of his own ethical and religious attitude which imperils modern Western man. One of the principal objects of this volume is to point out that a genuine moral attitude can only be born (if at all) out of reverence for the happenings in the human psyche.

I should like to take this opportunity of expressing my thanks to my teacher and friend, C. G. Jung, not only for the pioneer-ing work of a lifetime, on which my own work is based, but also for a large number of suggested corrections which I have been able to incorporate in this translation. I need hardly add that the responsibility for this volume remains entirely my own.

One final doubt. Is this new ethic which is supposed to be so essential for modern man "inopportune" at a time when the old ethic which prepared the way for it is so con-spicuous for being honoured in the breach rather than in the observance? I should like to answer this question by telling a Hasidic story.

On one occasion, Rabbi Jechiel Meir of Gostynin had attended the Festival of Weeks with his teacher at Kozk. On his return home, his father-in-law asked him, "Well, was the Revelation[1] received in a different spirit where you were than elsewhere?" "Certainly!" came the reply. "How do you mean?" asked his father-in-law. "How would you here understand, for example, the commandment 'Thou shalt not steal'?" asked Rabbi Jechiel in return. "Well, naturally," replied his father-in-law, "'one may not steal from one's neighbour.'" "They do not need to give *us* this commandment any longer," said Rabbi Jechiel. "In Kozk they interpret it as follows: 'One may not steal from oneself!'"[2]

Tel Aviv, 1959   Erich Neumann

[1] The revelation of the Law to Moses on Mt. Sinai—(*Trans.*).

[2] Martin Buber, *Tales of the Hasidim*, Zurich, 1949.

CHAPTER I

INTRODUCTION

"Near and hard to grasp is the God.
Yet, where peril lies,
Grows the remedy, too."
—Hölderlin

The problem of evil is one of the most central problems of modern man. No appeal to old values and ideals can shield us from the recognition that we live in a world in which evil in man is emerging from the depths on a gigantic scale and confronting us all, without exception, with the question: "How are we to deal with this evil?"

The modern age is an epoch in human history in which science and technology are demonstrating beyond doubt the capacity of the conscious mind to deal with physical nature and to master it to a very large extent — at any rate, to a greater degree than in any earlier period in human history. But it is also an epoch in which man's incapacity to deal with psychic[1] nature, with the human soul, has become more appallingly obvious than ever before.

The lake of blood which swallowed Europe and threatens to engulf the entire world — for the world wars are only a symptom of this condition — is the result of this incapacity.

The phenomenon which brands our epoch is a collective outbreak of the evil in man, on a scale never before manifested

[1] Note: "psychic" is used throughout this book as the adjective from "psyche" and not with any parapsychological connotation – (*Trans.*).

25

in world history. The various conscious explanations – ideological, political, sociological, etc. – which, as depth psychology knows, never grasp the real cause of the matter, cannot explain away the fact that it has been possible for evil to seize hold of hundreds of millions of human beings. The old ethic of the Judaeo-Christian epoch has proved itself incapable of mastering the destructive forces in man.

It can be shown that the decline of what we describe as the "old ethic" is a necessary phenomenon in human history. But this confronts us with the question as to whether the tendencies or basic features of a new ethic are already in existence, since the human race is in danger of being annihilated by the "moral insanity" which has taken possession of it and which is a symptom of a transitional period lacking an ethic.

It is only in appearance that the front lines in the conflict at present dividing mankind are clearly delineated. No doubt it is true that the combating of evil is not the same thing as evil itself; yet the fact remains that man's present state of possession by evil is a phenomenon that transcends political and military frontiers and enters into the hearts of each one of us, whatsoever our position may be. The murdered are also guilty – not only the murderer.

Those who saw and failed to act, those who looked away because they did not want to see, those who did not see although they could have seen, and those, too, whose eyes were unable to see – each and every one of these is actually in alliance with evil. We are all guilty – all peoples, all religions, all nations, all classes. Humanity itself is guilty.

The evil which broke through in the Nazis' claim to world dominion is the same evil which has hitherto prevented the solution of the social problem and the self-determination of the coloured peoples in the civilised world, and is attempting with all its might to destroy the reality of the unity of mankind and the consciousness of a single destiny for culture and the human race.

The people of our time are in an unenviable position. On the whole, they have nothing with which to confront the deliberate annihilation of the world by evil except an ethic which has already lost its psychological efficacy. The inner insecurity of the individual who relies on the values of the old Judaeo-Christian ethic, but no longer feels its validity in his heart and experiences its impotence in his everyday life renders him an easy prey to infection by evil.

We have all seen how not a finger is lifted on behalf of "the Good", unless that finger happens to belong to a body whose own existence is directly threatened. But this implies that individuals or peoples are not activated by the Good, even when those individuals or peoples subsequently exploit the ideology of goodness; they are activated simply by the instinct of self-preservation sparked off by danger. So long as evil does not threaten one's own existence it is hung about with all sorts of pretty little pretexts, and these are only torn away when it bares the teeth of naked aggression against oneself, one's own house or one's own country. It is not the fight against evil itself — such is the bitter truth of our experience — but at best the fight against annihilation by evil which incites modern man to take action.

We are inclined to assume that this reaction is a universal human characteristic and that it has always been the basic attitude of mankind. But we overlook the fact that there have unquestionably been periods in which men have taken the initiative spontaneously in the fight against evil and that this has actually led to mass movements. If such mass movements and initiatives are analysed, it can easily be shown that they have not only been double-crossed by opposing forces, but also that forces have always existed which have used goodness purely as a pretext for exploitation. Yet there can be no doubt that to the consciousness of the men of those times evil was in fact evil and the fight against this evil a "holy war".

So long as the old ethic remained valid, its values possessed living efficacy; however, since his picture of the world has been invaded by the breakthrough of the dark side, modern man has become so sceptical and unsure of himself in matters of value that he can no longer see himself as a fighter for good and against evil. He has lost the naivety of the fighter, and the secret question which undermines his inner confidence is this: "Who is fighting against whom, what against what?"

When man's religious orientation formed the background to his ethical orientation, he knew quite simply that Yahweh or Ormuzd, Christ or Allah had ordained the fight and with it the hierarchy of values. But the question as to whether "industry" or "class", "imperialism" or "nationality" or "race" is the driving force behind the conflict, as to whether the individual is deceived or ignorant about its causes because the driving forces behind it are camouflaged, or whether he is fighting without being aware of the disease of which these conflicts are really the symptom — this whole apparently insoluble question which has been given a thousand different answers lives in the consciousness of every combatant as an expression of the chaotic situation of our time.

The absoluteness with which the opposing ideologies offer themselves as a solution to this problem is admittedly a "help" to the conscious mind of the individual who can allow himself to be possessed by one of them. But the psychological law which requires that every fanaticism of the conscious mind shall be compensated by an equally powerful doubt in the unconscious explains why these ideologies have in fact contributed so much to the confusion of our time and so little to its reorientation.

The "old" ethic in its Judaeo-Christian form moulded the character of Western man. Its loss of efficacy is the cause, the effect and the expression of a catastrophe in which the opposing forces that were contained by the old ethic have become visible. But the rudiments of a new ethic which expresses the change in the basic psychic constellation of modern man can be detected on every hand.

The problem of evil confronts modern man in both a collective and an individual form. During the last hundred and fifty years of the history of Western man, it has broken through on the widest possible front. It has undermined and destroyed the old cultural categories, but its course can also be followed in detail in the psychological history of the individual.

The study in depth of the psychological development of the individual in whom the problem of evil becomes manifest is in a much better position than any research into collective events to detect those first attempts at a synthesis which are the basic elements of a new ethic. This is due to the fact that external collective developments are decades behind the development of the individual, which is like a kind of *avant-garde* of the collective and is concerned at a far earlier stage with the problems which subsequently catch the attention of the collective as a whole.

It is not difficult to understand why positive attempts at a solution appear earlier and are more easily recognisable in the development of the individual than in that of the collective. The individual who is brought up against the overwhelming problem of evil and is shaken by it, and often driven by it right up to the brink of the abyss, naturally defends himself against destruction. In order to survive at all, he needs, as a matter not of arbitrary choice but of urgent necessity, the aid of the forces of the deep unconscious; in them and in himself he may be able to find new ways, new forms of life, new values and new guiding symbols.

But this reality of evil by which the individual is possessed is not derived simply from his personal reality; it is also, at the same time, the individual expression of a collective situation. Similarly, the creative energies of his unconscious, with their hints at new possibilities, are not simply his own energies but also the individual form taken by the creative side of the col-lective — that is, universal human — unconscious.

Both the problem and the level at which the solution emerges are manifested in the individual; both, however, have their roots in the collective. It is precisely this that makes the experience of the individual so significant. What happens in him is typical of the total situation, and the creative stirrings which enable him to find his own solutions and salvation are the initial stages of future values and symbols for the collective.

The individual (and his fate) is the prototype for the collective; he is the retort in which the poisons and antidotes of the collective are distilled. That is why the deep psychic happening which seizes hold of an individual and reveals itself in him in a form that can be experienced has a special meaning for a period of transition and of the collective disintegration of standards.

The future of the collective lives in the present of the individual, hard pressed as he is by his problems — which can, in fact, be regarded as the organs of this collective. The sensitive, psychically disturbed and creative people are always the forerunners. Their enhanced permeability by the contents of the collective unconscious, the deep layer which determines the history of happenings in the group, makes them receptive to emerging new contents of which the collective is not yet aware. But these are also the people for whom problems become insistent in their personal lives a hundred years or more before the collective has woken up to their existence.

Just as the problem of woman was anticipated by the women of the romantic movement, so the moral crisis of the twentieth century was anticipated by Goethe in *Faust* and by Nietzsche — to take only two examples. But what is true of the creative individual is also true, to a lesser degree, of sensitive people and of some neurotics. Not infrequently a sensitive person falls ill because of his incapacity to deal with a problem which is not recognised as such by the world in which he lives, but which is, in fact, a future problem of humanity which has confronted him and forced him to wrestle with it.

This explains the lack of contemporaneity, the remoteness and the eccentric isolation of these people — but also their prophetic role as forerunners. Their fate and their often tragic struggle with their problems is of crucial significance for the collective, since both the problem and the solution, the criticism which destroys the old and the synthesis which lays the foundation for the new, are preformed by these same individuals for the collective, which in fact takes over their work.

The connection between the problems of the individual and those of the collective is far closer than is generally realised. We are still by no means always aware of the "totality constellation" by virtue of which each single individual is an organ of the collective, whose common inner structure he bears in his collective unconscious. In this structure, the collective is no abstraction but the unity of all the individuals in which it is represented.

The marital tragedy of the individual is the arena to which the problem of the changed relationship between man and woman is brought for settlement by the collective – a problem which has a collective meaning and relevance transcending the marital conflicts of the individual. And similarly, the moral problem which drives the individual into neurotic sickness is at the same time an arena and an expression of the fact that the collective is not grappling with the problem of evil which is actually clamouring for its attention.

So long as certain specific values retain their living efficacy and power in the collective, the individual (unless he is an exceptional person) will have no problems in relation to matters of value. He will not fall sick because of problems arising out of these values, since institutional procedures exist for dealing with questions of value in a valid way. So long as and so far as the sacrament of marriage exists, there will be no neuroses caused by the marriage problem, but only adultery and sin, punishment and pardon. The orientation remains valid even if the individual behaves invalidly.

But when the collective no longer possesses values, that is to say, when a crisis in values has occurred, the individual lacks a collective orientation. He falls sick because of a problem for which there is no longer a collective answer and a collective procedure for reaching a settlement. He then becomes involved in a conflict from which no institution is any longer in a position to set him free, but for which he must suffer and experience an individual solution in the living process of his personal destiny.

CHAPTER II

THE OLD ETHIC

The scope of what we describe as "the old ethic" is actually very wide. It comprises the most variegated human ideals and includes a whole gamut of degrees of perfection. But in every case it involves an assertion of the absolute character of certain values which are represented by this old ethic as moral "oughts".

The old ethic of the West has many sources, the Judaeo-Christian and the Greek being the most influential among them. It is not our task here to enumerate the origins and the various combinations and inflections of the old ethic or to trace the course of its development. The ideal prototype at the centre of the old ethic may be the figure of the Saint or the Wise Man, the Noble or the Good, the Devout or the Orthodox Fulfiller of the Law, the Hero or the Man of Self-control.

But whether the *kalos kai agathos* of the Greeks, the gentleman ideal of the English, the devotion of a St. Francis or the Pharisee's fidelity to the law appears as the dominant symbol, in every case a good which can be known is represented as an absolute value. This value may be regarded as a law which can be revealed or immanent, as an intuited idea or as the behest of reason, but it is always a codifiable and transmittable value which governs human conduct in a "universal" manner.

It is always held that the ideal of perfection can and ought to be realised by the elimination of those qualities which are incompatible with this perfection. The "denial of the negative", its forcible and systematic exclusion, is a basic feature of this

33

ethic. However variable its dominant symbols may be, the moral formation of the personality is in every case only made possible by a conscious tendency to one-sidedness and by insistence on the absolute character of the ethical value. This invariably excludes all those clusters of qualities which are incompatible with that value. It is not our concern here to investigate the validity of values (their relativisation has been one of the results of Western development) or to arrange them in an order of precedence. Our task is rather to study the psychological effects of this old ethic on Western man. It will then become clear that there are two basic principles – two basic methods, in fact – which have made possible the implementation of the old ethic. These basic methods are suppression and repression.

It is in *suppression*, that is to say, in the deliberate elimination by ego-consciousness of all those characteristics and tendencies in the personality which are out of harmony with the ethical value, that "the denial of the negative" is most clearly exemplified as a leading principle of the old ethic. Discipline and asceticism are the best-known forms assumed by this technique of suppression, which is used by the Judaeo-Christian and the Indian or Mohammedan saint to deny satisfaction to the needs of the body and of sexuality, by the faithful fulfiller of the Law to exclude all tendencies contrary to that law, and by the gentleman to refuse admittance to all those human characteristics which are incompatible with his ethical ideal.

Suppression is a conscious achievement of the ego, and it is usually practised and cultivated in a systematic way. It is important to notice that in suppression a sacrifice is made which leads to suffering. This suffering is accepted, and for that reason the rejected contents and components of the personality still retain their connection with the ego.

It is true that a moral veto which requires the suppression of a given type of instinctive reaction denies satisfaction to that instinct; at the same time, however, the suppressed instinctive reaction still continues to play an important part in the view of life held by the ego-consciousness that suppresses it. We shall consider the psychic economy of suppression when we analyse the psychic effect of the old ethic.

In contrast to suppression, *repression* may be regarded as the instrument most frequently used by the old ethic to secure the imposition of its values. In repression, the excluded contents and components of the personality which run counter to the domin-ant ethical value lose their connection with the conscious system and become unconscious or forgotten – that is to say, the ego is entirely unaware of their existence. Repressed contents, unlike those suppressed, are withdrawn from the control of conscious-ness and function independently of it; in fact, as depth psy-chology has shown, they lead an active underground life of their own with disastrous results for both the individual and the collective.

What the study of neuroses has demonstrated in the case of the individual, we shall now show is also true of the collective: the complexes of the unconscious which have been shut away from daylight by repression undermine and destroy the world of consciousness. The uncleanness and tangled obscurity of the situation which arises as a result of repression has effects which are actually far more dangerous than those of asceticism, with its clear conscious attitude of suppression.

The authority by whose aid the old ethic imposed its behests on the individual was "conscience", and this authority of con-science, as Spitteler had already pointed out in his *Prometheus and Epimetheus*, stands in an antithetical relationship to the "Voice", which is the individual expression of psychic truth. It is true that Freud did subsequently modify his earlier statement to the effect that conscience was originally "social anxiety" and "nothing else";[1] if, however, we take the difference between

[1] Sigmund Freud, "For the Times on War and Death" and *Civilisation and its Discontents*.

conscience and the inner voice as our starting-point, his statement can be seen to be justified.

To a considerable extent, the moral authority in man is conditioned by his environment, by society and by the age in which he lives. If he agrees with the canon of values which is dominant in the community and which constitutes the "cultural super-ego", he will be said to have a "good conscience". Disagreement with the canon, on the other hand, will involve the stigma of a "bad conscience". Conscience is the representative of the collective norm, and changes as that norm changes its contents and demands. In the Middle Ages, this collective authority demanded total agreement with the Old Testament view of the world, and condemned and suppressed the scientific approach as "heretical"; in the nineteenth century, the same authority required total agreement with the scientific view of the world, and condemned and suppressed religious tendencies as "priestly frauds". The same conscience forbids pacifism in the warrior caste and the aggressive instinct in a pacifist group.

The consciousness of the individual originally develops with the aid of the collective and its institutions, and receives the "current values" from it. The ego, therefore, as the centre of this consciousness, normally becomes the bearer and representative of the collective values current at any given time. The ego is in fact the authority which, in more or less complete identification with these values, represents the demands of the collective in the individual sphere and rejects any counter-tendencies that may be present.

The aim of the collective is always to achieve a way of life and of living together which is disturbed to the smallest possible extent by the forces operating in the individual, irrespective of whether these forces are of high or inferior value in themselves. Whatever is opposed to the equilibrium of the collective is tabooed, and its development in the individual is forbidden. It is, however, impossible to fix the content of the values which create this equilibrium. What constitutes a value for one society, period, or community, may represent an anti-value to another.

Agreement with the values of the collective is the ethical guide-rope thrown out to the individual members of the group; conscience is the endopsychic authority which attempts by its reaction to bring this agreement about. Freud's explanation of the super-ego as an introjected exterior authority is to that extent justified. However, complete agreement with the collective values in force at any given time is in fact impossible. As the values of the old ethic are "absolute" (that is, not adjusted to the reality of the individual human being), adaptation to these values is one of the most difficult tasks in the life of any individual. It is an essential part of his adaptation to the collective.

We have seen that suppression and repression are the two main techniques employed by the individual in his attempt to achieve adaptation to the ethical ideal. The natural result of this attempt is the formation of two psychic systems in the personality, one of which usually remains completely unconscious, while the other develops into an essential organ of the psyche, with the active support of the ego and the conscious mind. The system which generally remains unconscious is the shadow; the other system is the "façade personality" or persona.[1]

The formation of the façade personality represents a considerable achievement on the part of conscience. Without its aid, morality and convention, the social life of the community and the ethical ordering of society would never have been possible in the first place. The formation of the persona is, in fact, as necessary as it is universal. The persona, the mask, what one passes for and what one appears to be, in contrast to one's real individual nature, corresponds to one's adaptation to the requirements of the age, of one's personal environment, and of the community. The persona is the cloak and the shell, the

[1] C. G. Jung, *The Relations between the Ego and the Unconscious*, C.W.7.

37

armour and the uniform, behind which and within which the individual conceals himself—from himself, often enough, as well as from the world. It is the self-control which hides what is uncontrolled and uncontrollable, the acceptable façade behind which the dark and strange, eccentric, secret and uncanny side of our nature remains invisible.

A large part of education will always be devoted to the formation of a persona, which will make the individual "clean about the house" and socially presentable, and will teach him, not what is, but what may be regarded as, real; all human societies are at all times far more interested in instructing their members in the techniques of not looking, of overlooking and of looking the other way than in sharpening their observation, increasing their alertness and fostering their love of truth.

Every kind of restriction may be imposed by the collective. But whether it is a case of a taboo in a primitive tribe, a social convention or a moral prohibition, whether it is a question of not mentioning certain subjects or of not admitting certain facts, of behaving as if certain non-existent entities in fact existed or of saying things which one does not mean or not saying things which one does mean – every time it makes one of these demands the collective will be guided by certain principles which are vital to its development and to the development of consciousness. Without these values it could not exist—or such, at least, is its firm conviction.

The ego will receive the reward of moral recognition by the collective to the exact extent to which it succeeds in identifying with the persona, the collectivised façade personality—the simple reason being that this façade personality is the visible sign of agreement with the values of the collective.

The process of persona-formation can take place at different levels, depending on the calibre and type of the individual and of the age in which he lives. From this point of view, it makes no difference whether the persona-personality by means of which the ego identifies itself with the demands and values of society, class or tribe belongs to a medicine-man or a solicitor, a chieftain or a party functionary, a king or an artist. It is equally irrelevant whether the society which imposes this collective mask upon the individual is primitive or civilised, democratic or Fascist.

The contrast between "conscience" and the "inner voice" (which we shall be considering in detail later on) is evidence in support of our contention about the relationship between ethics and persona-formation. This contrast is most clearly exemplified in the founders of new religious or ethical movements; these were invariably "criminals", and it was inevitable that they should be treated as such. Abraham (who broke his father's idols into pieces), the prophets, Jesus and Luther (who in turn superseded the narrow religious nationalism of the Jewish people, the old Law, and Catholicism) – all these were regarded as criminals in exactly the same way as Socrates, who introduced "new gods", or Marx and Lenin, who set out to destroy the established order of society.

The revolutionary (whatever his type) always takes his stand on the side of the inner voice and against the conscience of his time, which is always an expression of the old dominant values; and the execution of these revolutionaries is always carried out for good and "ethical" reasons. Often enough – though by no means always, as the history of the heresies may teach us – the course of history eventually recognises these "criminals" of the inner voice as the forerunners of a new ethic. But this in no way alters the fact that the conscience of the new age – though itself partly shaped by the impact of many revolutionaries of the inner voice – invariably re-establishes a canon of dominant values and requires the individual to adapt to this canon in its turn by the formation of a façade personality.

On the authority of conscience, the persona excludes a number of psychic components. In part, these are repressed into the unconscious, but in part, too, they are controlled by the ego and consciously eliminated from the life of the personality. All

39

those qualities, capacities and tendencies which do not harmonise with the collective values – everything that shuns the light of public opinion, in fact – now come together to form the shadow, that dark region of the personality which is unknown and unrecognised by the ego. The endless series of shadow and Doppelgänger figures in mythology, fairy tales and literature ranges from Cain and Edom, by way of Judas and Hagen, to Stevenson's Mr. Hyde and the ugliest man of Nietzsche; again and again such figures have appeared and made their bow before human consciousness, but the psychological meaning of this archetype of the adversary has not yet dawned upon mankind.

The shadow is the other side. It is the expression of our own imperfection and earthliness, the negative which is incompatible with the absolute values; it is our inferior corporeality in contradistinction to the absoluteness and eternity of a soul which "does not belong to this world". But it can also appear in the opposite capacity as "spirit", for instance when the conscious mind only recognises the material values of this life. The shadow represents the uniqueness and transitoriness of our nature; it is our own state of limitation and subjection to the conditions of space and time. At the same time, however, it forms a part of the nuclear structure of our individuality.

The old ethic admits two reactions to the psychic situation created by conscience. Both are perilous, but they are so to different degrees and with different results for the individual. The situation which is more common and more familiar to the average man is that in which the ego identifies itself with the ethical values. This identification takes place by means of an identification of the ego with the persona. The ego confuses itself with the façade personality (which is of course in reality only that part of the personality that is tailored to fit the collective), and forgets that it possesses aspects which run counter to the persona. This means that the ego has repressed the shadow side and lost touch with the dark contents, which are negative and for this reason split off from the conscious sector.

Owing to its identification with the collective values, the ego now has a "good conscience". It imagines itself to be in complete harmony with those values of its culture which are accepted as positive, and feels itself to be the bearer no longer simply of the conscious light of human understanding but also of the moral light of the world of values.

In the process, the ego falls a victim to a very dangerous inflation — that is to say, to a condition in which consciousness is "puffed up" owing to the influence of an unconscious content. The inflation of the good conscience consists in an unjustified identification of a very personal value (that is, the ego) with a transpersonal value, and this causes the individual to forget his shadow (that is, his creaturely limitation and corporeality). The result is that the inevitable lack of complete harmony between the ego and the collective values is tacitly omitted from the reckoning.

Repression of the shadow and identification with the positive values are two sides of one and the same process. It is the identification of the ego with the façade personality which makes this repression possible, and the repression in its turn is the basis of the ego's identification with the collective values by means of the persona.

The forms which may be taken by this ethical façade range from genuine illusion and an "as if" attitude to sanctimonious hypocrisy and downright lying. These false human responses to ethical demands are not confined to any one historical period; yet it is a fact that this pseudo-attitude has appeared with especial frequency in the history of the West during the past hundred and fifty years. Actually, Western man's illusory self-identification with positive values, which conceals the real state of affairs, has never been more widespread than in the bourgeois epoch which is now coming to an end. In contrast to earlier periods, however, this illusion has now been exposed from many different points of view by the self-criticism of modern man.

The positivist belief in progress was one of the precursors of the First World War, and the arrogation of modern man, regarding himself as the meaning and evolutionary culmination of creation, was a prelude to the bestial arrogation of the Aryan *Herrenvolk* under National Socialism.

The illusions and mendacity of the collective, in war and peace, are both cause and effect of the illusions and mendacity of its individual members, who betray their pseudo-Christian, pseudo-humanistic, pseudo-liberal and pseudo-human attitudes in every sphere of life.

Ego-inflation invariably implies a condition in which the ego is overwhelmed by a content which is greater, stronger and more highly charged with energy than consciousness, and which therefore causes a kind of state of possession in the conscious mind. What makes this state of possession so dangerous — irrespective of the nature of the content which lies behind it — is that it prevents the ego and the conscious mind from achieving a genuine orientation to reality.

. All states of inflation and possession are accompanied by a restriction of consciousness. The clearest example of this is the *idée fixe*, when the ego is overpowered and dominated by a fixed idea, with the result that it ignores essential aspects of reality. The tyranny of the content by which consciousness is possessed leads to the repression of such elements in reality as are incompatible with the idea that has obtained "possession"; and the ignoring of these factors then results in disaster.

As is demonstrated by a wealth of historical examples, every form of fanaticism, every dogma and every type of compulsive one-sidedness is finally overthrown by precisely those elements which it has itself repressed, suppressed or ignored. The inflation of the ego is brought about by its identification with the collective values. What makes this inflation so disastrous, however, is not some intrinsic danger to be found in the nature of the

42

values themselves; it is rather that, by identifying his personal ego with the transpersonal in the shape of the collective values, the limited individual loses contact with his own limitations and becomes inhuman.

But the individual's essential non-identity with the transpersonal is in fact the basis of his life. The uniqueness and individuality of man is realised precisely by the self-differentiation of the creaturely and limited from the unlimited power of the Creator. In inflation, this basic situation is by-passed, and man becomes a chimera, a "pure spirit" or disembodied ghost.

This constellation, which may manifest itself in the form of dreams of flying or of becoming invisible, often enough has the same ending as the flight of Icarus, which in fact portrays this basic psychological situation in terms of the symbolic language of myth. The pinions of the inflated ego, which are secured by nothing stouter than wax, cannot tolerate the solvent force of the transpersonal sun on its all too high and giddy flight. The result is the fall of Icarus into the sea; the ego, which had imagined itself to be immortal, is destroyed by being swallowed up by the unconscious.

It is this lower element, the part disregarded by man's *hubris* and sinful pride, which is responsible for his downfall in the end; the repressed element, overlooked in the arrogance of the flight, ultimately takes its revenge.

The devouring sea is well-known to us from the symbolism of myths and dreams as an image of the unconscious. In mythology, it is axiomatic that the *hubris* of man should be punished by his downfall and by the revenge of the gods. But this axiom is the projection of a psychological law. Every inflation, every self-identification of the ego with a transpersonal content — and that is the precise meaning of *hubris*, in which man imagines himself to be equal to the gods — inevitably results in downfall; the transpersonal content (that is, the gods) annihilates the ego, which is no match for its superior power.

The mythological image depicts the consequences of inflation for the individual ego. Our present concern, however, is rather with the collective disasters which occur as a result of the behaviour required by the old ethic. Value-inflation is not the only method of carrying out the old ethic — even though it is the method most frequently chosen by the average man.

Originally, the old ethic was the ethic of an élite. It was the solution adopted by strong personalities, who desired to solve the ethical problem by means of suppression — that is to say, by the conscious denial of the negative.

The psychological situation of these élite groups exposes them to quite different perils than those of repression and ego-inflation; they themselves are in fact characterised by quite a different psychic constellation. In their case, the dehumanisation brought about by inflation is prevented by a psychic phenomenon which is connected with both suppression and sacrifice. It is prevented by suffering.

The ascetic tendency of the old ethic is always accompanied by the conscious suffering of the individual on the horns of his existential dilemma — his dichotomy into "two souls", the rejected part which is to be suppressed and the conscious mind with its affirmation of values. Whether this suffering takes the form of ascetic denial, heroic conquest, trusting devotion or loyal obedience to the Law is of secondary importance. In suffering, the basic human situation of limitation is accepted and realised. The impossibility of an identification of his personal ego with the transpersonal value is experienced by man as a living reality when he *suffers* the tension of his dual nature and the sacrifice of his rejected side.

The aim of the old ethic is expressed in the injunction "Man should be noble, helpful and good" or in variations on the following ethical predicates: devout, believing, brave, efficient, dedicated and sensible. As we have already repeatedly emphasised, the methods used to achieve this aim are the repression or suppression of all "negative" components. This implies that the old ethic is, basically, dualistic. It envisages a con-

44

trasted world of light and darkness, divides existence into two hemispheres of pure and impure, good and evil, God and the devil, and assigns man his proper task in the context of this dualistically riven universe.

The ego's function is to be the representative of the light side. This basic attitude may express itself in many different ways. It may be active or passive, extraverted or introverted, political or religious, philosophical or artistic – and so on. The ego may identify itself with the light side in the battle and try to act as its representative. It may also fight and suffer on its behalf. In either case, the dualistic world, with its typical split into light and darkness, comes to be reflected in man himself.

The individual is now essentially split into a world of values, with which he is required to identity himself, and a world of anti-values, which are a part of his nature and can in fact be overwhelmingly strong, and which oppose the world of consciousness and values in the shape of the powers of darkness.

The dualism of the old ethic, which is specially marked in its Iranian, Judaeo-Christian and Gnostic forms, divides both man, the world, and the Godhead into two tiers – an upper and a lower man, an upper and a lower world, a God and a Devil. This dichotomy is effective on the practical level in spite of all philosophical, religious or metaphysical declarations of ultimate monism. The actual situation of Western man has been essentially conditioned by this dichotomy right up to the present day.

The old ethic is based on the principle of opposites in conflict. The fight between good and evil, light and darkness is its basic problem. However the content of good and evil may change in the individual, the principle of contrasting opposites and their resolution through conflict remains the substance of the old ethic. The ideal figure of this ethic is always the hero, whether he takes the form of a saint who is considered to be identical with the principle of light – an illusion which is symbolised by the halo — or whether, as St. George, he subdues the dragon. The other side is always either completely exterminated or decisively defeated and excluded from life. And yet the battle of the opposites is eternal. It corresponds to the basic Iranian concept of the battle between light and darkness, since the repressed, suppressed and conquered darkness invariably rises again; the heads cut from the Hydra are invariably replaced.

Mankind is confronted with the strange and, for the old ethic, paradoxical problem that the world, nature and the human soul are the scene of a perpetual and inexhaustible rebirth of evil. Just as light cannot be extinguished by the superior power of darkness, so too there is no evidence to show that darkness can ever be abolished by any superior power on the part of light.

From the point of view of the average man, the old ethic was based on ego-inflation and repression; the pseudo-solution it provided involved an identification of the ego with the values of the collective. For the moral élite, on the other hand, the position was more complicated. In their case, we find the opposite constellation — that is to say, a *deflation* of the ego. This deflation (an identification with the negative value, with evil) took the form of an overwhelming sense of sin, and found its classic formulation in the actual doctrine of original sin, or "Evil is man from his youth up".

There is a real possibility here that the devaluation of the ego may be so complete and the feeling of inferiority to the transpersonal power so catastrophic that there is really no significant place left for an ethic at all. Man's subjection to evil is in this case experienced as so unmitigated that nothing that man can do or be could possibly redress the balance. The only cure is in fact redemption by an act of grace on the part of the Godhead.

This extreme and one-sided attitude of identification with evil is succeeded by many other grades and stages in the consciousness of sin. To begin with, it is experienced as a more or less hopeless state of affliction by the earthly, material, corporeal and bestial side of life. This later moves on to an intermediate position. Man now at last arrives at some experience of his dual nature, which is good and evil at the same time. Yet here, too, the main stress is laid on the suffering caused by one's own evil side (which has to be suppressed), and "life in this world" — as understood, for example, by Puritanism and Pharisaism — becomes austere, gloomy and anti-vital in character.

It is typical of this attitude that ego-inflation and self-identification with the ethical value can flourish side by side with the depression caused by a consciousness of sin. The arrogance of inflation which "knows" the good, and the over-weening assurance that one has "done good" in one's practical life can coexist with the humility of a deeply contrite sense of sin.

In this psychology, all kinds of admixtures can in fact be found, from moral illusionism and the fulfilment of the Law as a reflection of one's own righteousness, to militant commitment in the battle for the good, intense suffering at the dualism of the world, despair at the evil of one's own heart and a self-corroding consciousness of sin. In any case, however, the experience of suffering imparts a dark background to life, and in this way the suppressed element makes its return and does indirectly touch consciousness.

By contrast with repression, in which all contact with the dark contents which cause suffering is destroyed by the splitting-off of the unconscious components, suffering permits the suppressor to live a comparatively normal life. He is not, like the repressor, attacked and overwhelmed by the dark forces of the uncon-scious. Voluntary self-limitation by sacrifice and suppression is a way of life which does not necessarily make the individual a sick person. For the collective, however, the consequences of this suppression are disastrous, even where the individual escapes injury. There is in fact this much common ground

47

between the two methods of suppression and repression: in both cases the collective has to pay for the false virtue of the individual.

Suppression and, still more, repression result in an accumulation of suppressed or repressed contents in the unconscious. From the point of view of the economy of energy, the advantage lies once again with suppression. An element that is suppressed always continues to play a part in consciousness in the form of a problem that disturbs the conscious mind. The fight against evil occupies a considerable proportion of the attention of consciousness. The ego, too, makes a definite sacrifice of psychic energy to the suppressed elements. In fact, the energy expended in suppression is to some extent a psychic equivalent for the non-realisation of the suppressed content. The energy which would have had to be invested in the realisation of this content is now made over to the same content in the form of the energy required for its suppression. What amounts to an equivalent quantum of energy remains bound to the rejected content and is invested in the inhibitory, blocking and holding mechanisms which are the instruments of suppression.

From the point of view of the development of consciousness, this kind of battle with the unconscious is partially justified. But neither the transfer of an energy-equivalent nor conscious preoccupation with the suppression nor the experience of the suppressed elements through suffering are adequate techniques for mastering the psychological problem caused by the suppression of ethically rejected — that is, evil — components of the personality.

In repression, on the other hand, even the partial assimilatory processes, the equivalents and the safety-valves which are to be found in suppression are lacking. Forces and contents which are completely repressed and have no means of access to consciousness do not remain unaltered in the unconscious or retain their original character: they change. The repressed contents become "regressive" and subject to negative reinforcement. It is not possible to discuss the process of regression in this context.[1] What can, however, be said here is that in regression more primitive forms of reaction are mobilised. For example, homicide committed in a burst of passion is a primitive form of reaction which has been overcome owing to the growth of consciousness (in the shape of conscience) and the development of law and justice. In regression, these higher forms of consciousness disintegrate and are replaced by the earlier primitive reaction.

It is a matter of common experience (which we cannot discuss in detail now) that contents which are capable of becoming conscious but whose access to consciousnessness has been blocked become evil and destructive. We know from daily life that the inability or unwillingness to admit the existence of a fact or content or to "abreact" something, as it is called, often makes a mountain – or rather an earthquake – out of a harmless molehill. The content which has been split off from consciousness becomes regressive and contaminated with other primitive, negative contents in the unconscious, with the result that, in an unstable personality, a minor irritation denied access to consciousness is not infrequently blown up into an access of fury or a serious depression. In quite general terms, it can be stated that forces excluded from the conscious mind accumulate and build up a tension in the unconscious, and that this tension is quite definitely destructive.

What, then, is the fate of all those personality components, stirrings, forces and instincts which are shut out from life by the old ethic? The more dogmatically the old ethic is imposed on individuals and societies – that is, the stronger the influence of conscience – the more radical will be this exclusion and the greater the split between consciousness with its value-identification, and the unconscious, which by way of compensation will take up the opposite attitude.

Where there is suppression, conscience shows its strength in

[1] See Jung, *On Psychic Energy*, C.W.8.

49

the shape of a conscious feeling of guilt; where there is repression, this feeling will be unconscious. The guilt-feeling is attributable, in either case, to the apperception of the shadow; but whether it appears openly in the form of suffering or remains unconscious depends, as we have said, on whether suppression or inflation and repression have occurred.

This guilt-feeling based on the existence of the shadow is discharged from the system in the same way by both the individual and the collective – that is to say, by the phenomenon of the *projection of the shadow*. The shadow, which is in conflict with the acknowledged values, cannot be accepted as a negative part of one's own psyche and is therefore projected – that is, it is transferred to the outside world and experienced as an outside object. It is combated, punished, and exterminated as "the alien out there" instead of being dealt with as "one's own inner problem".

The way in which the old ethic provides for the elimination of these feelings of guilt and the discharge of the excluded negative forces is in fact one of the gravest perils confronting mankind. What we have in mind here is that classic psychological expedient – the institution of a scapegoat. This technique for attempting a solution of the problem is to be found wherever human society exists.[1] It is, however, best known as a ritual in Judaism. Here the purification of the collective was carried out by solemnly heaping all impurity and evil upon the head of the scapegoat, which was then sent away into exile in the wilderness – to Azazel.[2]

The unconscious psychic conflicts of groups and masses find their most spectacular outlets in epidemic eruptions such as wars and revolutions, in which the unconscious forces which have accumulated in the collective get the upper hand and "make history". The *scapegoat psychology* is in fact an example of an early, though still inadequate, attempt to deal with these

[1] Cf. *The Golden Bough*, by J. G. Frazer.
[2] Lev. 16:8 (R.S.V.)—(*Trans*).

unconscious conflicts. This psychology shapes the inner life of nations just as much as it does their international relationships. Often the outbreak of mass epidemics and the scapegoat psychology are interconnected psychological reactions which stem from a single unconscious conflict. From the point of view of the final outcome, it is a matter of comparative indifference whether the conflict in question was not yet ripe for consciousness or whether it was one which had been previously repressed.

On the primitive level, where the consciousness of the individuals who make up the collective is still relatively weak, progress in the direction of the values necessary to society can be achieved in no other way than by the external projection of the shadow. At this stage, evil can only be made conscious by being solemnly paraded before the eyes of the populace and then ceremonially destroyed. The effect of purification is achieved precisely by the process of making evil conscious through making it visible and by liberating the unconscious from this content through projection. On this level, therefore, evil, though not recognised by the individual as his own, is nevertheless recognised as evil. To put it more accurately, evil is recognised as belonging to the collective structure of one's own tribe and is eliminated in a collective manner—for example by the High Priest transferring the sins of the people to the scapegoat as a vicarious sacrifice.

A purification of this kind will retain its psychological validity so long as the collective still feels identified with the vicarious sacrifice and is genuinely moved by it—so long, that is, as the immolation of the victim has not been debased to the status of a mere spectacle.

At this stage, the scapegoat psychology is still dominated by ethics at their most primitive level—that is, by group responsibility and group identity. It is true that in Judaism at a later date the individual is also involved as such in the purification by the confession of his sins and is in this way made aware of the existence of his shadow side. Even at that stage, however, the confession is not individual, but is born out of the spirit of collective responsibility, since each individual castigates himself for the sins of the collective and proclaims, "*We* have sinned, we have betrayed," etc.

For primitive man — and the mass man in every nation reacts, as we know, like a primitive man — evil cannot be acknowledged as "his own evil" at all, since consciousness is still too weakly developed to be able to deal with the resulting conflict. It is for this reason that evil is invariably experienced by mass man as something alien, and the victims of shadow projection are therefore, always and everywhere, the aliens.

Inside a nation, the aliens who provide the objects for this projection are the minorities; if these are of a different racial or ethnological complexion or, better still, of a different colour, their suitability for this purpose is particularly obvious. This psychological problem of the minorities is to be found with religious, national, racial and social variations; it is, however, symptomatic, in every case, of a split in the structure of the collective psyche. The role of the alien which was played in former times by prisoners of war or shipwrecked mariners is now being played by the Chinese, the Negroes, and the Jews. The same principle governs the treatment of religious minorities in all religions; and the Fascist plays the same part in a Communist society as the Communist in a Fascist society.

In the economy of the psyche, the outcast role of the alien is immensely important as an object for the projection of the shadow. The shadow — that part of our personality which is "alien" to the ego, our own unconscious counter-position, which is subversive of our conscious attitude and security — can be exteriorised and subsequently destroyed. The fight against heretics, political opponents and national enemies is actually the fight against our own religious doubts, the insecurity of our own political position, and the one-sidedness of our own national viewpoint.

It will continue to be necessary for the collective to liberate itself by exploiting the psychology of the scapegoat so long as there are unconscious feelings of guilt which arise, as a splitting phenomenon, from the formation of the shadow. It is our subliminal awareness that we are actually not good enough for the ideal values which have been set before us that results in the formation of the shadow; at the same time, however, it also leads to an unconscious feeling of guilt and to inner insecurity, since the shadow confutes the ego's pipe-dream that it is identical with the ideal values.

It follows that any kind of situation which is calculated to inspire us with confidence that our life is really in harmony with these values will be sought after and exploited. But the simplest way of achieving this object is to exterminate the shadow in the figure of the scapegoat.

The second class of people who play the part of victims in the scapegoat psychology are the "ethically inferior" — that is to say, those persons who fail to live up to the absolute values of the collective and who are also incapable of achieving ethical adaptation by the formation of a "façade personality". The ethically inferior (who include psychopaths and other pathological and atavistic persons, and in effect all those who belong psychologically to an earlier period in the evolution of mankind) are branded, punished and executed by the law and its officers. That at all events is what happens when it is not possible for this class of people to be made use of by the collective. In wartime, on the other hand, they are eagerly exploited.

This class, too, is treated as alien and exterminated as a foreign body, since that is the most spectacular way of bringing home to the collective its own otherness and difference from evil. The solemnity with which the extermination of evil is carried out by the collective is derived from the original collective significance which the sacrifice of the scapegoat actually possessed on the primitive level. The representatives of Church and State take part in the execution of judgement on the unfortunate victims of the scapegoat psychology in the fullest pride of a "good conscience"; and the relief felt by both individual and collective at the elimination of the "evil out there" is palpable in every case.

That these two classes of scapegoat victims are interchangeable — that not only is the evil man experienced as alien but that the alien, in his turn, is experienced as evil — is one of the basic facts of human psychology. It is a leitmotif which can be traced uninterruptedly from the psychology of primitives right down to the policy towards aliens of contemporary, so-called civilised states.

There is yet a third class of persons who are singled out to be victims by the scapegoat psychology — though they stand in the sharpest possible contrast to the class of the morally inferior which we have just described. This third class of victims consists of personalities who are actually superior — for example, leaders and men of genius. Many social customs provide illustrations of the primitive tendency to make a ritual, vicarious sacrifice of the best and most outstanding personality and to exploit him as a scapegoat for the expiation of the sins of one's own collective. This is probably the connecting link between the totemistic vestiges which Freud misunderstood as "patricide", the ritual murder of the king in the earliest days of human history and the doctrine of the sacrificial death of the suffering god.

There are two interconnected motifs here. The representative capacity of the outstanding personality also qualifies him to serve as a representative sacrifice on behalf of the collective before the face of "the Powers". At the same time, however, from the collective's point of view, the outstanding personality is regarded once again as an alien element. The occupants of marginal positions — whether they are inferior personalities who fall below the collective average or superior personalities who have the temerity to rise above it — are sacrificed by the masses, whose basic indolence makes them unwilling to budge from their own position at the centre.

Normally, the history of the so-called civilised nations is also

54

characterised by the sacrifice of certain outstanding individuals, though these are in fact the concentrated fulcra of power by whose action history itself is carried forwards. Socrates, Jesus and Galileo were alike members of this unending series. All nations and all periods of time have contributed to this scapegoat sacrifice of the outstanding, even if the ritual is nowadays no longer conscious but unconscious – a somewhat doubtful piece of progress.

Whether this reaction is the revenge taken by the collective for the exacting and in fact excessive cultural demands made on it by the outstanding personality is a question which we cannot examine here. It is, however, essential to realise that the unconscious shadow element from which the collective is attempting to liberate itself with the aid of the scapegoat psychology has its fling once again in the very cruelty which accompanies the sacrifice of the scapegoat – though the collective remains unconscious of this relationship. True to the basic principle of the scapegoat psychology, the conscious mind believes itself to be identical with the higher values and commits the most appalling atrocities in the sublime self-assurance of an "absolutely clear conscience". All wars (and in particular, all wars of religion), all class wars and all party conflicts provide examples of this coexistence between a good conscience in the conscious mind and a breakthrough of the shadow on the level of action.

We must distinguish here between two classes of persons – the suppressors of the shadow side, who combine an ascetic and heroic attitude to life with a conscious feeling of guilt and with suffering, and the repressors, in whom both the feelings of guilt and the suffering caused by them remain unconscious.

In both classes we find, as a consequence of the denial of the negative, an unconscious reinforcement of the negative in practice to the point of sadism and a bestial lust for destruction. The difference between them is simply this: in the ascetic class, the sadism is nearer to consciousness and assumes a rationalised

55

and systematic form, whereas in the repressive class, the masses, it is of the wildest emotionality and overwhelms consciousness.

Puritanism and the Inquisition, the legalistic Judaism of the Pharisees and the parade-ground discipline of the Prussian mentality are all subject to the same psychological law. The severity of the ascetic attitude is compensated by an aggressive sadism which finds its outlet in the institutions controlled by the leading ascetics.

A group which is psychologically split by being consciously identified with ethical values and at the same time unconscious of its shadow will display, in addition to unconscious feelings of guilt, a psychological sense of insecurity which is a compensation for the self-righteousness of its conscious attitude. Repression will have to be continually on the defensive against a dawning apperception of the shadow side, since the unconscious reinforcement of the shadow will make it increasingly difficult for the ego and the conscious mind not to become aware of its existence at some point in the process.

The inner split caused by this apperception of the shadow will then lead to an unconscious feeling of inferiority and to reactions of the kind discovered by Alfred Adler. The feeling of inferiority will be over-compensated by a tendency to exaggerated self-vindication and will culminate in a reinforcement of the repression. The projection of the shadow will now become systematised, and the final result will be the paranoid reactions of individuals and whole nations, whose own repressed aggressive tendencies reappear in the shape of fear of persecution at the hands of other people and of the world at large. Slogans such as the policy of encirclement, the conspiracy of the Elders of Zion, the white, black or yellow peril, the drive for world domination of capitalism or Bolshevism, etc., and all paranoid systems of this kind serve only one purpose – to repress the aggression and the shadow side of their originators.

Within the collective, this type of self-righteousness found expression in traditional methods of education and penal justice. Here too we meet the compromise of the scapegoat psychology, which under the pretext of ethical conduct allows its own shadow to have its fling by inflicting punishment, torture or deterrence. Appalling scope for the operations of the archetypal shadow is in fact provided, in varying degrees, by such institutional expressions of the ethical collective as executions, sentences of hard labour, prisons and penal establishments of every kind, probation – and even school and family life. All law which is based on punishment, that is to say, not on the knowledge that the collective itself is a party to the guilt of every evil-doer, is nothing but lynch law, under another name.

The institutional form of the scapegoat psychology is used by the task-masters of the old ethic (that is, by the ruling ascetics) primarily as an instrument of culture and civilisation; its emotional side, on the other hand, plays a far more significant and indeed catastrophic role in human history. The institutions of the scapegoat psychology no longer possess their original orgiastic character, which made it possible for them in former times to redeem the collective from its shadow problem by such devices as the holding of a ritual execution in the presence of the whole tribe. In these circumstances, there is an urgent and redoubled need for the collective to liberate itself from the aggressive drives which have accumulated within its bosom by some form of violent and explosive discharge; in this way, at least some transient relief can be obtained from the tension caused by these dammed-up energies. The resultant outbursts, which partake of the character of mass epidemics, wreak their fury on the scapegoat classes in the collective. At the same time, however, that basic phenomenon of the scapegoat psychology which we have described as the projection of the shadow also plays a decisive part in the international disputes between collectives which are known as wars.

No war can be waged unless the enemy can be converted into the carrier of a shadow projection; and the lust and joy of warlike conflict, without which no human being can be induced actually to fight in a war, is derived from the satisfaction of the unconscious shadow side. Wars are the correlative of the old ethic, and warfare is the visible expression of the breakthrough of the unconscious shadow side of the collective.

We find the same psychological constellation at work here as in the case of the individual. Any nation which is possessed by the inflation of a good conscience "knows" itself to be identical with the highest values of humanity; in fact, it identifies itself with these values and prays with a good conscience to "its God", as the undiluted quintessence of the light side, who is of course in duty bound to award it the victory. But this inflation by the good conscience is not in the slightest degree disturbed by the acting out of a bestial shadow.[1]

This split between the world of ethical values in the conscious mind and a value-negating, anti-ethical world in the unconscious which has to be suppressed or repressed generates guilt feelings in the human psyche and accumulations of blocked energies in the unconscious. Naturally, these are now hostile to the conscious attitude, and when they finally burst their dams they are capable of transforming the course of human history into an unprecedented orgy of destruction.

The old ethic must be held responsible not only for the denial of the shadow side but also for the creation of the resultant split, the healing of which is now of crucial importance for the future of humanity. The further progress of mankind will in fact depend, to no small degree, on whether it proves possible to prevent the occurrence of this splitting process in the collective psyche.

[1] Today, it is true, certain differences may already be discernible between the nations; the total bestial unconsciousness of repression may in fact coexist with a somewhat greater degree of awareness, which recognises the negative element in destruction as negative and accepts it with a new kind of moral responsibility.

CHAPTER III

STAGES OF ETHICAL DEVELOPMENT

If we are to understand why the situation of the old ethic has become critical in our own time, and why it is particularly in the last hundred and fifty years that events have culminated in a disintegration of the old values and a progressive disorientation of modern man, of which we ourselves are both eyewitnesses and victims, we shall have to devote some brief consideration to the evolution of consciousness and its various stages in the human species. The evolution of ethics and the evolution of consciousness are closely interrelated, and it is not possible to understand one without the other. We have described the stages in the evolution of consciousness at length elsewhere,[1] and we can only retrace the broad outlines of this evolution here, without going into details.

The starting-point of the whole development is the stage of "primal unity". In this stage, the embryonic ego, an ego which is still largely helpless and dominated by the unconscious, lives in a condition of almost complete dependence on the tribe, the world and the collective unconscious. "Participation mystique" and the dominance of the collective psyche over the still

[1] See *The Origins and History of Consciousness*, by the present writer, translated by R. C. F. Hull, New York (Bollingen Series XLII) and London, (Routledge) 1954. In this work, the ideas about the psychology of culture which are employed in the present volume fall into place in the context of a systematic account of the evolution of human consciousness and culture. The *specific purpose* of the present volume is to demonstrate the relevance of the psychology of culture to ethics.

undifferentiated individual psyche are the most striking characteristics of this primal human situation. As is only to be ex-expected, there is no individual or conscious ethical responsibility in this primary stage of ethical development. Since the individual only functions as a member of the group, and group consciousness is more important than individual consciousness,[1] not unnaturally we always find also group responsibility and a group ethic at this level. The condition of participation mystique, of the unconscious mutual identity of persons, is expressed in the fact that the group is responsible for the individual and that each individual, for his part, is regarded as an incarnation of the whole group. Primitive psychology abounds in behaviour-patterns which reveal how the group is identical with its constituent members and how, in turn, each single individual represents the whole group in his own person.

Whatever happens to the individual happens at the same time to the whole group, and the whole group reacts as such to what happens to any individual member (cf. the phenomenon of the blood feud). Responsibility is located not in the individual but in the group. And just as the whole group is regarded as affected by an act of murder, so too it is not the intention of the group to strike back at the *individual* murderer. As the whole group to which the murderer belongs is guilty, blood revenge can be exacted from any given member of it.

The unconscious mutual identity of the members of a group can be carried to the point where, for example, the murder of parents or of a brother may remain unavenged because the murderer has, so to speak, made an attack on his own flesh. He and his closest relations are practically identical. The interests of the group are in no way affected — any more than they are in the case of a suicide. And the interests of the group are the only thing that matters. In the same way, the damages due for the murder of a distant relative will be less than those required for the murder of a stranger — though the principle

[1] L. Lévy-Bruhl, *The "Soul" of the Primitive.*

of liability is itself recognised. By virtue of his group identity, the murdered relative is part-property of the murderer. On the other hand, in China, for example, we find the reverse conclusion drawn from this identity: the parents and the responsible family grouping are punished for an offence committed by a son.

The belief held in classical Judaism that Jahweh may reward or punish a man's descendants for that man's own acts belongs to the same group of ideas. From the ethical point of view, this presupposes that the group identity of the family persists through the generations; it implies that it is not only contemporary members of the clan who are felt to be a group, but that the family's descendants in line also constitute a unit – a concept which is of great importance for the understanding of Judaism.

The reality of group identity is not only demonstrable from the biological angle – it is also a psychological fact. This fact is repeatedly confirmed by the analysis of modern individuals. Not infrequently, the neurosis or pathological reactions of an individual are attributable to some "guilt" on the part of his parents or even grandparents, and the effect of this guilt continues to operate so long as it remains unconscious. To take only one example, a grandfather's strictness may be responsible for a lack of independence on the part of his daughter; the daughter's subsequent reaction when it comes to educating her own children may then turn the latter into neurotics.

In the primal stage, when the individual members of the group are still to a large extent undifferentiated, the "Great Individual" will represent the mana-personality[1]; he will be, in a sense, the Self of the group, its creative centre, and it will be from him in his capacity as leader and creator that the collective will receive its values.

As we have explained elsewhere,[2] the Great Individual acts as a founder and initiator in every sphere – that is to say, he is

[1] See *The Relations between the Ego and the Unconscious*, by C. G. Jung, C.W.7.
[2] Op. cit. Appendix I: The Group and the Great Individual.

a spiritual progenitor. He performs this function as a doer of mighty deeds and a hero, as an artist, a scientist, a philosopher, a religious leader – and also as the founder of an ethic.

Ethical values are created as a result of a revelation by the "Voice" to the Founder Individual. We can trace this source of the collective ethic in revelations to Founder Individuals throughout human history, from primitive man right down to civilised nations. The utterances of gods, the decisions of seers and medicine-men, priests, chiefs and the divinely possessed, from oracles and judgements delivered by a god to the revelation of the deity in a god-given law – all these are unique acts of revelation born out of a particular situation. At a later date, they are collected and codified and endowed with an abstract and universal validity – and in the process, they become divorced from the concrete situation in which they were originally revealed.

The basic constituents of a given ethic are derived from the "Voice" which speaks to certain favoured individuals. Their unique spiritual gift consists precisely in the fact that it is they who hear the Voice. Whether the Voice belongs to a god or a beast, a dream or a hallucination, the reality of this Voice is absolute and binding so far as the Founder Individual is concerned. It derives either "from God" or else from a symbol which represents God, and it is later taken up by an élite which the Founder personality gathers around himself and is subsequently imposed by them as a collective standard on the whole tribe.

The creative individuals who found ethics display the equivalent religious and ethical attitudes in their own personal lives. In the actual process of foundation, however – that is, when the ethic revealed by the Voice is transmitted by the Founder to his élite of disciples in the form of a law – this individual religious ethic is transformed into a collective ethic.

The élite then proceeds to educate the collective in the principles of this new ethic, and represents its values as universal

62

and binding on all mankind – that is to say, as collective values which the tribe has to incorporate in its own life.

We find this attitude of the outstanding individual, which is based on the inner revelation of the Voice, not only among primitives but also among the great founders of religions, who have always imposed a new ethical burden on the community in which their ideas took root.

The typical course of ethical development proceeds by way of the original revelation to the Great Individual and the identification of the élite with that revelation, to the stage of the collective ethic in which the group accepts "the Law" and acknowledges it as binding upon itself, the contents of the law being irrelevant in this connection. In the final phase, the collective subjects itself to the ethical canon uncritically and with the same kind of matter-of-fact certitude which unreflecting people always display in the face of any established institution. For a mind without historical consciousness, custom is custom and law law, for the simple reason that it always has been so; and even this rationalisation is only the answer to a question put by the Western enquirer to the primitive, and not by the primitive to himself.

Subjection to the collective law does, however, represent an important advance in consciousness. It implies that the evolution of consciousness has reached a stage when the primal unity, and, with it, the tyranny of the unconscious, is broken up, and the differentiation and strengthening of the ego and the conscious mind lead to a separation between the two systems of consciousness and the unconscious. This separation between the systems is connected with a general development of trends and functions which seek to strengthen the consolidation of the conscious mind and its demarcation from the unconscious. The influence of the collective ethic operates in the same direction.

At the level of primitive man, the social life, education and progress of the tribe are disturbed and obstructed by the tyranny of unconscious forces. Here the law, representing a collective standard which focuses attention on the light side of the conscious mind and the ethical values associated with it and declares war against the powers of darkness, is performing an absolutely necessary function. The collective value-system proclaimed by the élite in their capacity as executors of the Founder Personality is invariably to be found ranged on the side of consciousness and against the tyranny of the overpowering dominants of the unconscious.

The old ethic liberated man from his primary condition of unconsciousness and made the individual the bearer of the drive towards consciousness; so long as it did this, it remained constructive. Even when it takes the primitive form of a fixed collective canon of morals, the ethical imperative "Thou shalt" may actually assist the development of consciousness; it may, in fact, provide a general framework of orientation which will act as a breakwater against the emotionality of man's unconscious, with all its elemental, incalculable power.

This explains why it was that the old ethic played an important ancillary role in the evolution of human consciousness. It represents an essential transitional stage, and its techniques of suppression and repression are an integral part of the defence-mechanisms of the conscious mind against the unconscious. Actually, it is true to say that a certain devaluation and deflation of the unconscious are urgently needed in the initial stages of the developmental process; the conscious mind is still very weak, and without this tendency to devalue the unconscious it could never have established and consolidated its position or proved its value as a formative agency in the creation of culture.

On the primitive level of magic, for example in the ritual of the scapegoat sacrifice, the mystery drama in which evil is paraded before the eyes of the worshippers is an initial phase in the process of making them conscious. Here everything is acted out externally, on the objective level, which is the screen for the projection of the inner drama. As in the case of classical tragedy, the subject of the happening is the experiencing collective, not the individual. The experience of evil externally and in an alien figure provides the basis for the formation of conscience as an internal authority and representative of the collective values. But the process of the formation of conscience as an internal psychic authority is an expression of the individualisation of group man, even though the contents of conscience are still not individual but collective.

The development of the ego and of consciousness is subject to the potent formative influence of the collective. In its initial phase, ego development does not involve the deve' pment of a creative ego but of an ego that is capable of carrying out and applying the demands of the collective, on itself as well as others, independently and under its own motive power – and this involves fulfilling the commandments and prohibitions of the collective ethic with the aid of its own individual conscience.

As the individual and his ego-consciousness are progressively differentiated and separated out from their matrix in the primitive collective, human development proceeds to a second ethical stage – the stage of individual moral responsibility. To begin with, this individual responsibility expresses itself within the framework of the collective ethic – that is to say, the individual attempts to put the values of the collective into practice or to identify himself with them.

Since they realised that the development and differentiation of consciousness was a tendency that was necessary for the progress of the human race, the élite attempted in this phase to eliminate all trends that ran counter to the old ethic. Even if (as we have seen) their attempt was unsuccessful, they did succeed in creating the conditions for a partial extension of human consciousness in the interests of development as a whole.

Before the appearance of the old ethic, the ego had remained to a large extent a victim of the unconscious forces which had now come to be forbidden. It was subject to and dominated by these forces and instincts, which took possession of it in the form of sexuality, lust for power, cruelty, hunger, fear and superstition. The ego was their instrument and was totally unaware that it was in fact possessed, since it lived them out blindly and was unable to interpose any kind of distance between itself and the power which had taken possession of it. But for an ego which is required to accept responsibility, this stage of unconsciousness and possession amounts to a sin.

At this stage, the old ethic demands the recognition of these contents and their suppression. Suppression is one of the typical acts of that process of self-differentiation and self-distancing which provides the initial basis for psychological consciousness. That part of the psyche which previously represented a dominant that "drove" the ego now becomes — to some extent at any rate — a content of consciousness and the centre of a process of argumentation and conflict in which the ego confronts this part of the psyche in a subject-object relationship. Even when the ego morally fails, sins, and is overwhelmed by the content which it was supposed to suppress, it no longer enjoys the primitive condition of undifferentiated unity which was characteristic of the pre-moral state of "being driven"; it knows very well that — and what — it ought to have suppressed. It has eaten of the Tree of the Knowledge of Good and Evil. The moral stance of consciousness remains intact even when the ego fails.

The collective ethic which, with its doctrine of individual responsibility to conscience, represents the classical form of the old ethic, then continues to evolve in two directions. Both these directions correspond to analogous processes in the development of the ego and of the consciousness of the individual.

The first leads, with the progress of individualisation, to the "ethic of individuation", the "new" ethic; the second, to the collapse of the old ethic and to regressive phenomena which we have described elsewhere.[1] And just as, in the evolution of

[1] Op. cit. Appendix II: Mass Man and the Phenomena of Recollectivization.

66

man as a whole, the hero is the prototype of the development of the individual,[1] so too the founder of an ethic is the prototype for what can happen in each single individual today.

The revelation of the Voice to a single person presupposes an individual whose individuality is so strong that he can make himself independent of the collective and its values. All founders of ethics are heretics, since they oppose the revelation of the Voice to the deliverances of conscience as the representative of the old ethic.

The psychological law of the relativity of ethical revelations states that the individual revelation to the élite company of disciples is imposed on the collective, and that collective man then introjects the revealed law in the form of the authority of conscience, while at the same time all those forces and tendencies which run counter to the revelation are suppressed or repressed.

Each new "thrust" of revelation – that is to say, each new self-revelation of the Voice in an individual – is opposed to conscience as the representative of the old collective ethic. It is therefore inevitable that the ethical revelation delivered to the creative individual will be in advance of the collective and will in fact represent an ethical level often far beyond the normal ethical level of the collective. This antinomy is insoluble. By the founding act of the pioneer individual, the collective is given a law which will lead, in the course of history, to its further development, but which is, at the time, beyond its reach.

Even though, today, we have reached the point of no return for the old ethic, we should do well to remember how much it has contributed to human progress in the past; we should also remember that (subject to one restriction for which we shall give our reasons later) it continues to be valid even now for a considerable part of the human race. At the same time, the regressions which disfigure this story of progress show quite clearly that the old ethic in its legalistic form actually makes

[1] Op. cit. Part I: The Mythological Stages in the Evolution of Consciousness.

excessive demands on the majority of human beings. In fact, ways and means will have to be found of preventing the occurrence of the negative effects of these excessive demands; otherwise, the legalistic requirements of the élite lead inevitably to a disastrous splitting process. On the one hand, we have the select company of those for whom the law handed down by the founder corresponds to their own nature and ethical development — whether this élite consists of medicine-men, priests, warriors, philosophers or saints, of prophets or the disciples of prophets; on the other hand, we have the group upon which the canon of values is "imposed" as a law, and which, although it accepts this law, is in fact still below the level of its requirements. And while it may be true to say that the élite can meet the demands of the ethical canon without injury by making use of such techniques as suppression and sacrifice, asceticism and self-discipline, the effect of these same demands when imposed upon the collective may be nothing short of catastrophic. This is a danger which has never been sufficiently recognised.

The élite creates a human ideal which the collective recognises as its highest value and attempts to realise in practice. But the collective, which is made up of average people, possesses a far more primitive psychic structure, in which the very forces and tendencies which it is supposed to overcome are particularly strong and active — far stronger, at any rate, than they are in the élite. The collective can in fact only conform to the ideal requirements of the old ethic as proclaimed by the élite by making the most violent efforts — if at all.

It is at this stage that we witness the onset of the process described above — identification with the ethical values, formation of a façade personality and repression into the shadow side of all personality components inconsistent with those values. This leads to a paradoxical situation. The individual, in his capacity as a member of the group, is set at variance with the values of the collective, which are now expressed in terms of the new moral ideal. This is collectively binding and collectively

68

recognised, although it has in fact been imposed on the group by the legislative fiat of the élite and runs counter to the nature of the collective.

This would amount to an incomprehensible paradox if it were not for the fact that the élite and the personality of the ethical Founder do actually represent an essential stage forwards in development. Because this is the case and because – to mention only one example – the assumption of judicial authority by the State and the community represents an advance in comparison with blood feud, there is a natural tendency, which exists even in group man, to accept the higher law of the élite. In the process, however, he represses, or at best suppresses, all those tendencies in his nature which run counter to the new ethical establishment.

This development is reinforced by the ethical rigorism of the élite, which imposes the demands of the new ethic upon the collective with the same severity as upon itself. Though this may appear to serve the interests of moral progress, it actually reinforces the splitting tendencies within the collective to a dangerous extent. And the psychic split produced by the new ethic in turn gives birth to the scapegoat psychology and the violent eruption of the repressed side in the form of mass epidemics.[1]

[1] The problem of the group under the pressure of a moral standard which is too high for it has always existed, but it was counterbalanced in earlier times by a group identity which was still effective. Even when the unity of the tribal collective, with its original group responsibility, had ceased to exist, the village commune, the guild and ultimately the family were still there to play the part of the collective. The collective was in a position to assimilate its weaker brethren, who were below the cultural level of the period and its values; it was able to neutralise them or to take care of them without their constituting a collective problem. The village idiot and the cripple, the madman and the dullard continued to live in the community, irrespective of whether the group identity consisted of tribe or class, village commune or family. This situation continued to prevail so long as groups remained small and a strong consciousness of group identity existed.

In recent centuries the development of consciousness and individualisation reinforced the individual ethic of a growing élite, released ever-increasing numbers of people from the original anonymous group responsibility, and led them on to the stage of individual moral responsibility; yet the highest obligation still remained the acknowledgement of canonised collective values.

At the opposite pole to this trend towards individuality, we find the *"recollectivisation" process* of modern times, which came about as a result of the unprecedented expansion of the species *homo sapiens* during the last few centuries. Recollectivisation has led to the break-up of the traditional groupings. From the point of view of the old ethic, masses are by nature inferior; they tend to revert to the primitive group-identity which involves no individual responsibility – that is to say, they behave in an atavistic and regressive manner – while at the same time they are not included in any form of comprehensive group responsibility either.

Within the context of this process of recollectivisation, larger and larger aggregates of people fall below the cultural standard of the élite and are violated by the demands of the old ethic. The larger a mass of people is, the lower, by a necessary law, must be the average level of consciousness, culture and morality. The result is the growth of an increasingly numerous class of people who fail to reach the standard set by the élite, and are therefore branded as antisocial, inferior, depraved or criminal.

The efforts made by this class to suppress or repress their incompatible tendencies provoke an activation of the negative unconscious side in both the individual and the group. The result is a growing discrepancy between the moral level of the individual and the ethic of the collective.

The accumulation of repressed contents in the "recollectivised" collective threatens to disintegrate the old Judaeo-Christian ethic, and the nihilistic and materialistic movements which arise as a result of this crisis actually tend to undermine the basis of individual responsibility itself.

The growing split between the conscious mind of mass man and his repressed shadow side leads in the first place to the kind of stiffening of the persona and concealment of the difference between what is actually achieved and what is demanded by the old ethic which became notorious in the form of the hypocrisy and deceitfulness of the nineteenth century, and particularly of the Victorian age.

If, however, the distance between nature and the demands of the élite grows too wide, even the pseudo-solution of conscious identification with collective values becomes impossible.

In the last few centuries, this fate has in fact overtaken increasing numbers of human beings. These are people whose psychological make-up is incompatible with the ethic of the élite – people, very often, who possess a psychology which would have been normal in previous ages and whose level of consciousness fails to correspond with the historical epoch in which they live.

Such cases of atavism are only extreme examples of the unevenness of development which we normally find in modern man. This betrays itself in many ways – for example, as a technologist he may be living in the present, as a philosopher in the period of the Enlightenment, as a man of faith in the Middle Ages and as a fighter of wars in antiquity – all without being in the least aware how, and where, these partial attitudes contradict each other.

At this stage in the argument, it is necessary to expose the erroneous idea of the equality of man, as seen from the psychological point of view. At the same time, however, the kernel of truth concealed within this error must be safeguarded against all possible misunderstanding. The kernel of truth in the idea of the equality of man has to do with the equality of human nature. We are only just beginning to understand that this identity of human nature at the deepest level has its roots in the collective unconscious.

The collective unconscious is the precipitate of all identical and original reactions of the species *homo sapiens*. It is that which makes man man, in contrast to every other species of animal. The continuing identity of man's primary reactions, as these are revealed in the instincts and archetypes, is a correlate to the structure of his psycho-physical system, with its tension between the opposing poles of the autonomic and cerebro-spinal nervous system, the belly-soul and the head-soul.

In contrast to this identity of structure at the deepest level, however, we find the most marked inequality of structure at the level of the conscious mind. This inequality is observable not only as between races (for example, the negroes and the major white races and nations), but also as between tribes, families and individuals.

It is a fact that constitutional differences in endowment and in capacity for development in general and for the development of consciousness in particular may cover an extremely wide span. Heredity and training, collective influences and individual temperament are here intertwined in a complex play of affinity and opposition. And yet, to prevent all possible misinterpretation, it has to be recognised that – especially in an era of social injustice – the principle of the equality of man does provide a basis for asserting the right of the individual to personal development and for demanding that obstacles placed in the path of this development by unjust external circumstances should be eliminated, once and for all.

It is certainly true that a juster social order, based on the equality of man, could make it possible for larger élites to develop from the broad masses of mankind. But this does not in any way impugn the justice of our contention that human beings are in fact unequal and that modern "recollectivisation" merely exacerbates the split between the élite and an increasing number of people who are unable to satisfy the requirements of the élite and find themselves at variance with them.

The excessive demands made by the élite on the collective and the resultant blockage of the repressed shadow side in the unconscious is an extremely modern and novel ethical problem. We are, in fact, witnessing the emergence of an ethic which no longer considers the ethical attitude and decisions of the individual in isolation, and which does not simply evaluate that individual's conscious alignment, but which also takes into account the effect of this alignment on the collective, and includes the situation of the unconscious in the overall moral assessment.

When we speak of a new collective ethic, we do not, of course, mean by this the regressive tendencies which are observable nowadays and which reconstitute the collective ethic of primitive man and attempt to destroy individual responsibility. On the contrary, we mean that the progressive ethical development of the individual must also take into consideration the effect of his ethical attitude on the collective.

Side by side with the "responsibility before God" which constrains the individual to attend to the "Voice", we have to place his "responsibility before the community". This responsibility is no longer confined, as it used to be, to the task of converting the ethic of the Voice, which is binding on the individual, into a general ethic by legislative fiat. The individual is no longer responsible for himself alone, and for his success in fulfilling his own ethical demands, but, in so far as he generalises his attitude, he must also admit his responsibility for its unconscious repercussions on other people, who may be at a lower intellectual, human and ethical level than himself.

As a result, we have an ethic of a relativistic and hierarchical character, which does justice to the advanced individualisation of modern man and his marked tendency to variations in type. The aim is to avoid the psychic split characteristic of the old ethic, and in so doing to eliminate one principal cause of very

73

many individual cases of mental sickness and pathological development; at the same time, this will have the effect of removing one crucial precipitant of mass epidemic eruptions of the shadow side of human nature.

A large part of the background of the new ethic and many of its individual features are already beginning to emerge and become clearly visible, though the full portrait has still to be completed. However, before we turn to this subject, we will repeat in summary form our conclusions about the old ethic.

Psychologically speaking, the old ethic is a partial ethic. It is an ethic of the conscious attitude, and it fails to take into consideration or to evaluate the tendencies and effects of the unconscious. It is typified by the text from St. Augustine in which the saint thanks God that he is not responsible to him for his dreams.

The old ethic demands suppression and sacrifice, and in principle, also admits of repression — that is to say, it does not consider the condition of the psyche or total personality, but contents itself with the ethical attitude of the conscious mind, a partial system within the personality. In terms of the collective, this encourages an illusory form of ethics, orientated solely towards the action of the ego and the conscious mind. This is, in fact, a dangerous illusion: in the social life of the group and the collective, it leads to negative compensatory phenomena in which the repressed and suppressed shadow side breaks through. Within the life of the community, this takes the shape of the psychology of the scapegoat; in international relations it appears in the form of those epidemic outbreaks of atavistic mass reactions known to us as wars.

The old ethic has not only proved inadequate as a solution to modern man's most pressing moral problem; it also confronts him with an additional hazard due to the splitting tendency brought about by its dualistic conception of the world and of values.

The partial ethic is an individualistic ethic, since it accepts no responsibility for the unconscious reactions of the group or the collective. That is why the old ethic is inadequate; the compensatory relationship between consciousness and the unconscious which it fails to take into account turns out to be a major cause of the contemporary crisis in human affairs and actually the crucial ethical problem of our time.

The ethical demand that responsibility must be accepted even for unconscious processes is clearly derived from the problematic psychological situation of modern man as an individual. Even in terms of the collective, however, the same problem is thrusting its way into the foreground, since no élite can impose its ethic on the masses without bringing upon itself the resultant catastrophe.

In modern man, the process of "recollectivisation" and its polar opposite, individualisation, have lead to great differences in ethical level, and this in turn has resulted in such an intensification of psychic tension in both individual and collective that this whole situation requires for its solution a new development of consciousness and a new ethic.

CHAPTER IV

THE NEW ETHIC

We now have to consider the problematic situation and the moral crisis of the individual, and to understand the processes which, in his case, mark the transition to the new ethic. We must return to the relationship between the collective and the individual which we emphasised at the beginning, and to the connection between the problems of the collective and the fate of the individuals in whom these problems are exemplified.

The conflict or disease which compels a modern man to embark upon a course of depth psychology is very seldom of such a kind that a simple correction of the conscious attitude, a mere rearrangement of the given material along the lines of a new structural pattern, is sufficient to bring about a solution. In most cases it proves necessary to open up, and make available to consciousness, levels of the personality which had previously been beyond the range and span of its experience and were for that very reason termed "unconscious".

In former times, a crisis of this nature was experienced as a threat to the soul's salvation. For example, the commission of a grave sin was a matter of such importance to a man's consciousness that it threatened his entire existence, his "soul" and the innermost citadel of his life. Modern man, on the other hand, experiences his situation in the first place as nothing more than a crisis affecting his conscious mind and his ego. The conflict is interpreted as a breakdown, a defeat, a failure to deal with a specific situation or vital problem; but man scarcely ever feels himself imperilled or challenged in the totality of his being. In most cases, he only feels that the integrity of his ego has been called in question, and he defends himself energetically against the realisation of the scope and range of his real problem.

The journey of depth psychology, which retraces the path between this situation and its origins in the background and underground recesses of the personality, always and inevitably leads to a severe disturbance of the ego and the world of consciousness. The reason is simple: in the course of this journey, the world of consciousness is confronted with the totality of the personality and with the boundless realm of the unconscious.[1]

Whether a man approaches the work of depth psychology in the light of an experience which has already taught him that his view of the world, his moral code and his manner of life are unequal to the impact of the problems which beset him, or whether the inadequacy of his previous orientation is only revealed in the course of the analysis, the fact remains that a severe disturbance in his world of values is almost always to be expected at the outset of the journey of depth psychology.

Almost without exception, the psychic development of modern man begins with the moral problem and with his own reorientation, which is brought about by means of the assimilation of the shadow and the transformation of the persona.[2] We are describing this process in the terminology of the analytical psychology of C. G. Jung, since this gives the most completely differentiated account. It can, however, quite easily be transposed into the terminology of Adler and Freud — at least in its initial stages.

[1] We are concerned here, as always when we speak of the psychological journey, only with those people for whom the process of individuation is a necessity — that is to say, mainly with people in the second half of life whose adaptation to the collective has already been made.

[2] C. G. Jung, *The Relations between the Ego and the Unconscious*, C.W.7.

The moral problem raised by the journey of depth psychology is most clearly formulated in the concept of the "shadow personality". As Jung recognised, the zone of the shadow and the confrontation with this figure is to be found at the beginning of the psychological journey. This then leads through the whole hierarchy of the zones of the psyche, all of which must be duly experienced in any true development in depth.

The disillusioning effect of the encounter with one's own shadow, the unconscious negative part of the personality, is always to be found in cases where the ego has lived in identification with the persona and the collective values of the period. That is why this encounter is, as a rule, particularly severe and difficult for the extravert, since by nature he has less insight into his subjectivity than the introvert. The naive self-illusion of the ego, which has more or less identified itself with everything good and fine, receives a severe shock, and the undermining of this position forms the essential content of the first phase of the analysis.

It is extraordinary to observe in how many cases this illusory attitude of the ego has been by no means destroyed by the crisis or neurosis which has led to the analysis. The absence of a "sense of sin" (that is, of a moral reaction to the shattering experience which has disrupted one's life) appears to be a characteristic of our own time.

In earlier periods, sickness or failure was experienced in terms of the categories of sin, guilt and punishment; this moral reaction, however, is generally alien to the consciousness (not the unconscious) of modern man. Nowadays the situation is thought of largely in terms of exposure to outside influences — other people, circumstances, the environment or heredity — in relation to which the personality is a "victim".

The popular causalistic conception of psycho-analysis, according to which certain very early childhood experiences are regarded as the "cause" of a later failure, plays very much into the hands of this attitude, and is in fact an expression of it.

The result is that in a crisis the ego feels itself innocent since it cannot identify itself in a really responsible way with the ego of early childhood.

In the encounter with the shadow, however, the ego falls out of its persona-identification with the values of the collective. The reductive analytical work of Freud and Adler went to great lengths to expose the shadow side of the human psyche, in all the starkness of its contrast to the illusory self-evaluation of the ego. The encounter with the "other side", the negative component, is marked by an abundance of dreams in which this "other" confronts the ego in such guises as the beggar or cripple, the outcast or bad man, the fool or ne'er-do-well, the despised or the insulted, the robber, the sick man, etc. etc.

But what shakes the individual to his foundations is the inescapable necessity of recognising that the other side, in spite of its undoubted character of hostility and alienness to the ego, is a part of his own personality. The great and terrible doctrine of "That art thou", which runs like a leitmotif throughout depth psychology, first appears, on a painful and most discordant note, in the discovery of the shadow.

The individual is driven by his personal crisis into deep waters which he would usually never have entered if left to his own free will. The old idealised image of the ego has to go, and its place is shaken by a perilous insight into the ambiguity and many-sidedness of one's own nature.

A process in which the ego is compelled to recognise that it is evil and sick in mind, antisocial and a prey to neurotic suffering, ugly and narrow-minded – an analytical technique which punctures the inflation of the ego and obliges it to experience exactly how and where it is limited and one-sided, conditioned by its type, prejudiced and unfair – all this represents such a bitter form of self-encounter that one can readily understand the resistance that it arouses.

To be obliged to admit that one is infantile and maladjusted, miserable and ugly, a human animal related to the monkeys, a sexual beast and a creature of the herd is in itself a shattering experience for any ego that has identified itself with the collective values. But the roots of the shadow problem go deeper still, and it becomes a matter of deadly earnest when the probe reaches right down to the sources of evil itself, where the personality experiences its relationship with the enemy of mankind, the drive to aggression and destruction, in the structure of its own being.

In the end, the individual is brought face to face with the necessity for "accepting" his own evil. To begin with, this statement may appear unintelligible; it is certainly true that its full significance can by no means be realised at the first glance. The act of the acceptance of evil should not be minimised or disguised by any attempt at relativisation which may try to reassure us by pretending that this evil which has to be accepted is not so bad, after all; and the situation is not made any easier by the fact that evil no longer appears in the form of a collectively recognised phenomenon.

"My" evil may not be an evil at all in my neighbour's eyes, and vice versa; it is precisely this that constitutes the moral difficulty of the situation. Group valuation and group responsibility cease at the point where no approval by the generally accepted standard can take away the ego's insight that it has acted in an evil manner, and where, on the other hand, no condemnation by the collective has either the power or the right any more to replace the ego's own orientation.

The differentiation of "my" evil from the general evil is an essential item of self-knowledge from which no-one who undertakes the journey of individuation is allowed to escape. But as the process of individuation unfolds, the ego's former drive towards perfection simultaneously disintegrates. The inflationary exaltation of the ego has to be sacrificed, and it becomes necessary for the ego to enter into some kind of gentleman's agreement with the shadow — a development which is diametrically opposed to the old ethic's ideal of absolutism and perfection.

This process of coming to terms with the shadow leads in fact to an apparent moral levelling-down of the personality. The recognition and acceptance of the shadow presupposes more than a mere willingness to look at one's dark brother — and then to return him to a state of suppression where he languishes like a prisoner in a gaol. It involves granting him freedom and a share in one's life. But the process of allowing the shadow to take part in one's life is only possible on a "deeper" moral level. The ego is obliged to step down from its pedestal and realise the state of individual, constitutional and historical imperfection which is its appointed fate.

The acceptance of one's own imperfection is an exceedingly difficult task. Each one of us, irrespective of his psychological type and sex, has an inferior function and a shadow; that is why we all find the assimilation of this side of the personality equally difficult.

If, in a dream, a hunchback springs over the hedge and flings himself at the dreamer's throat with the cry, "I too want a share in your life!" the violence and robberlike character of the shadow seems overstressed. But wherever the ego shows itself unwilling, the shadow will be driven to use violence; this means that violent contents, which are at first alien and unknown to ego-consciousness, will break through in the reaction which the ego experiences from the unconscious. In this case, the problem of the shadow and the moral conflict confront the ego in the disguised but aggressive form of the activation of a complex. The reduction of neurotic sickness by Freud and Adler to the instincts of sex or power is based precisely on the fact that the shadow breaks through in a symptom or complex.

It is a natural temptation to reject this kind of "acceptance of the negative" as a senseless, unnecessary or even dangerous process, and to maintain in the first place that the lowering of the ego's status brought about by the acknowledgement of the shadow is only permissible or necessary in exceptional "pathological" cases. Yet in fact, this lowering of the ego's status is neither an arbitrary matter nor an isolated incident but an expression in individual terms of the collective situation of our culture. In contrast, say, to the Christian man of the Middle Ages or to ancient, Asian or primitive man, Western man is at present in a position where there is an actual collective lowering in the status of his ego which has to be accepted and assimilated. The breakthrough of the dark side into Western consciousness is, in fact, an irreversible process.

By the *breakthrough of the dark side* into Western consciousness we understand that whole complex of parallel developments which has led, in the course of the last hundred and fifty years, to the phenomenon of "darkness" becoming visible and problematic in widely different areas at the same time. This process is bound up with what we have described as the recollectivisation of Western culture, which has resulted in a reinforcement of collective phenomena and a clear precedence of collective over individual happenings.

The breakthrough of the dark side corresponds to a basic shift of the psychological centre of gravity in a downward direction, towards the earth, on such a scale as has never previously been experienced by the Christian world of the West. The discovery of the "ugliest man", of the unhappy, the evil and the primitive occupies a far larger part of the ground in the cultural life of our time than we normally realise.

This discovery of the primitive element in human nature is the decisive factor in the situation. The world of the primitives, of the dawn of mankind and the earliest stages of human history have now placed man in a new perspective against the background of the world and the cosmos; they have shown him the dark soil in which his roots are embedded and appear radically to have destroyed his godlike nature and to have unmasked his central position in the universe as an illusion.

Man's "conditioning by nature" – his heredity and constitution, the mass man and the instinctive substructure of the individual, the unconscious as a decisive determining factor –

all these elements, with their surprising unanimity and undeniably far-reaching repercussions on the status of the individual ego, seem to point in the same direction: the recognition of the dark side. Darwin's "proof" of man's kinship with the apes, Biblical criticism and the thesis which interprets spirit as an epiphenomenon of the economic process, Nietzsche's *Beyond Good and Evil,* and Freud's *Future of an Illusion* – all these have contributed to the destruction of the old values. Secularisation, materialism, empiricism and relativism are the key concepts which exemplify this shift in the centre of gravity – particularly as contrasted with the Christian man of the Middle Ages and his orientation to the world.

In no previous epoch of human history has the dark side occupied the foreground of attention to such an extent as it does today. The sick, the psychopath and the psychotic, the degenerate and the cripple, those in need of care and attention, the abnormal and the criminal arouse the interest and sympathy of contemporary man as never before. Research workers and even State-run public institutions are beginning to concern themselves with such classes of people, often in a spirit of fascinated absorption which appears almost perverse when contrasted with the lack of interest shown in normal people and *their* misery.

In conformity with this general trend, ugliness, dissonance and evil are now forcing their way into art. The road which leads from Mozart via Beethoven to atonality in music and the corresponding processes of disintegration and transformation in literature and painting are expressions of the decline of the old order of life and values in the realm of aesthetics. This is by no means simply a question of the great revolutionaries such as Dostoievsky, in whose work man – sick, evil and abandoned – stands naked at the very heart of despair. The universal phenomenon of detective stories, crime films and thrillers belongs to the same uncanny context.

It would, of course, be an exaggeration to claim that no

previous ages have ever witnessed this side of human nature. The religions of redemption – Christianity among them – have always appealed to this element. But whereas previous ages regarded the depths of man's nature as evil and in need of redemption, and yet at the same rejected and banned them and sought to extrude them from the canon of values, today this side of life is the source of a deep, uncanny and perilous fascination. This fascination of modern man by the dark side "requires" something of him and should by no means be overlooked or explained away. Its darkness may be perilous, but it also contains the germs of any possible future development in the West – even though the manifestations of disaster and disintegration undoubtedly occupy the foreground in the initial stages.

Nowadays, Western man is aware that he is conditioned by biology, history, sociology and psychology; he realises his dependence on his own body, his dependence, too, on political and economic realities, and for this reason he is pervaded by a profound sense of the insecurity of his ideological and intellectual position. It is true that, at the level where he is an individual in possession of an ego, he is not always fully conscious of this dependency (in fact this is the real danger of the situation); yet this feeling pervades the whole atmosphere of his life and is the basis of his existential insecurity. The tyranny of the collective and the experience that his personal constitution is conditioned at every point undermines the position of the individual, and a mass psychology which denies the significance of individual personality in principle deprives the ego of its last vestige of support and self-confidence.

This is particularly liable to happen when the structure of the ego and the conscious mind is also experienced as dependent on a psychological unconscious which at every point and in every case proves its overwhelming superiority to the ego. With a few heroic exceptions, however, individual man in the West never became personally conscious of this breakthrough of the dark side until the advent of depth psychology. On the contrary, the Western inflation of the ego – that trend which has been so vehemently pursued by European civilisation since the time of the Renaissance – still colours the individual's philosophy of life. This means that the feeling or obscure intuition of an existential peril and insecurity coexists with the "certainty" of an ego which believes that it can do, know and organise everything and which rejoices in the motto, "Where there's a will there's a way". The polarisation of these opposite positions – the self-assurance of the ego on the one hand and the ever-increasing pressure of the dark side on the other – leads finally to a split in the personality of both the individual and his group.

This collective disorientation of modern man, especially when it remains unconscious and unassimilated – that is to say when it does not become a personal experience of the individual – gives rise to a series of dangerous reactions which have decisively moulded the general ethos of our age and the personal lives of our contemporaries.

Two main types of reaction can be distinguished, and, by a typical quirk of the psyche, both may occur jointly in the same individual.

The first reaction is deflationary and collectivist, and devalues both the individual and the ego. The second is inflationary and individualistic. Unlike the first, the second reaction overestimates and overvalues the individual and the ego. Both represent unconscious attempts to escape from the real problem. Common to both is the desire to conceal the fact that a new ethical attitude is called for to deal with the conflicts by which modern man is oppressed.

The first response to the disintegration of the old value-system is nihilistic and negativistic; it includes a variety of different ways in which human self-respect can be defeated. The ideal of the blond beast, the principle that "consciousness is a disaster",[1] and the ideology of blood and soil are variants of this fatal reaction. Common to them all is the "knowledge"

[1] Seidel, *Bewusstsein als Verhängnis*.

that the value-system of consciousness is bogus and the hostility to consciousness which is the reaction to this "insight". If the value-system of consciousness is an illusion, it follows that renewal through consciousness is impossible and that the attempt to achieve it must be abandoned. The result is an identification of the ego with collective anti-values which contrasts with the ego-identification with collective values that was typical of the old ethic.

Consciousness and knowledge then become pseudo-values; and whereas only recently (for example, in the psychology of Alfred Adler) the unconscious was regarded as a trick (that is an appendage) of consciousness, the nihilistic reaction reduces consciousness in its turn to a trick of the unconscious. Consciousness is now seen simply as a means for the realisation of unconscious instinctive forces, and spirit and knowledge are regarded as no more than instruments in the hands of various instinctive constellations belonging to the group or to individuals within it.

This nihilistic reaction is a radical form of the tendency to materialism, which is yet another symptom of the breakthrough of the dark side in the Western world. The various forms of materialism in philosophy also result in a reduction and deflation of human self-respect, since consciousness and spirit and the realm of values are construed as epiphenomena of a substructure belonging to a different order. Just as, in sociology, values are regarded as mere ideologies and superstructures of "real" basic conditions, so, in psycho-analysis, cultural phenomena are interpreted as mere "unreal" compromise products of a psychic structure which is basically unconscious.

In either case, a pessimistic and deflationary philosophy of this kind is an expression of the deep disturbance of consciousness brought about by the experience of the shadow side of life. But whereas the Judaeo-Christian ethic experienced the opposites in a dualistic manner, by suffering, or by combating the "other" side, the nihilistic reaction is negatively monistic – that is to say, it reduces the principle of the opposites to a single (e.g. materialistic) basic structure and explains the spiritual side as an epiphenomenon.

The other, inflationary mode of reaction is also monistic — but in this case the value-sign is reversed. It could be described as pleromatic mysticism. It is a view of the world which has attracted a great deal of attention in our own time. It involves an attempt to disregard reality in its character of existent givenness. It is "pleromatic" in the sense that the pleroma, the fullness of the divine nature as it was before the world began, when the Godhead had not yet entered into the world, is regarded as the "real" state of the world. It is mystical because relationship or relatedness with the pleroma can only be achieved in a mystical or illusory manner.

The pleromatic mystical reaction is generally to be found in conjunction with eschatological elements — that is to say, with tendencies towards a Utopian anticipation of a state of redemption which in the history of religion has normally been looked forward to as coming at the end of time. It contains remnants of the old ethic, but the driving force is provided by an eschatological psychology of achieved redemption which believes that it has already attained a state of being beyond the opposites. The ego attempts to evade the problem of the darkness and the shadow side of the world and of man in an illusory way by means of a mystical, inflationary expansion of the individual, who equates himself with the pleroma, the primal spirit, the Godhead, etc., soars into the realm of the infinite and the absolute and loses his identity in the process. A classic contemporary example of this attitude is provided by Christian Science, which simply denies the existence of the negative — but something very similar is to be found in many mystical, sectarian and political movements.

The pleromatic and the nihilistic attitudes to the shadow problem of modern man are often found in conjunction with each other, a liaison which we find prefigured in many Gnostic sects. The pleromatic mystical tendency is most clearly exemplified in those collectivistic movements which claim to provide redemption, and which actually do so in a certain sense, since they regard the individual as pleromatically fulfilled and in so doing raise him to a state of achieved redemption. In this way the individual is recollectivised – that is to say, reduced once again to a collective component of the mass; at the same time, however, he is redeemed from his isolation, since his individual responsibility is taken away from him. The liberation of the individual from his moral problems and the assumption of responsibility by the collective is the real basis for the redemptive character of all collective movements. Nowadays, this redemptive character generally takes a political form, but it is not difficult to see how, in this case, politics is the "opium of the people", and, in fact, a substitute for religion.

Faith in the dogma, the leader and the redeemer contains such a strong component of pleromatic fulfilment that the moral problem appears to be solved – and this leads, by way of the recollectivisation and disintegration of individual consciousness, to the moral insanity of the collective as the ultimate result of the pleromatic mystical reaction.

This phenomenon is most clearly exemplified in National Socialism, but political fanaticism and collectivisation produce similar phenomena wherever they appear. The leader-figure is identified with the redeemer-figure, the mana-personality of the collective unconscious,[1] and his teaching is imposed as a doctrine of salvation. Once this doctrine is accepted, the function of individual consciousness as the authority for the decision of moral questions is replaced by the mana-personality, and the substitute redeemer-figure is identified with the primal spirit which transcends all moral values. As a result, human personality disintegrates, the shadow is forgotten, and the individual is reduced to a phantasm and driven into the arms of mental illness. This phenomenon is known to us from the psychology of

[1] C. G. Jung, *The Relations between the Ego and the Unconscious*, C.W.7.

religious mania, and in our own period a whole host of similar collective phenomena can only be understood along the same lines.

Both the nihilistic and the pleromatic reactions tend towards a monism in which the attempt is made to abolish the principle of the opposites that constellates the moral problem and to exalt one of the two poles to the status of an absolute. In the nihilistic reaction, the spiritual side is reduced to an epiphenomenon of matter; the pleromatic outlook, on the other hand, considers spirit to be the sole real existent and the material world to be its epiphenomenon, which can in fact be disregarded at will. From this view, the world becomes something very much like an error in perspective.

Finally, there is one more form of reaction to the insistent demands of the shadow problem which should perhaps be mentioned. This is the attempt to remain free of all moral values and to conceive of life in terms of behaviourism or libertinism or utilitarianism. It is an attempt to shut out the world of darkness once again, and, by so doing, to evade the inescapable crisis of consciousness which is involved in any real effort to take the problem of evil seriously.

This type of non-reaction usually appears in a mixed form – that is, compounded with the other attitudes. It tries to eliminate the moral problem by adopting a kind of ostrich policy towards evil, partly by reducing it to material terms and partly by projecting it on to other conditions. It is typical of this attitude, too, that man does not take evil upon himself as a problem – and yet in practice he still allows it the fullest freedom of operation.

The two flight-reactions to the shadow problem – the collectivistic and the individualistic-pleromatic-mystical – represent extreme attempts at identification with one member of the pair of opposites which make up the conflict – the mass and the élite. In collectivism, it is ego-consciousness and the world of values which are sacrificed; in the pleromatic mystical trend, it is mass man and the shadow.

89

Neither reaction is in fact able to abolish or resolve the reality of the shadow problem which modern man is required to deal with. Owing, however, to the instability of their protagonists, both the collectivist movement, with its tendency to nihilism, and its pleromatic counterpart, which is coloured, very often, by the illusions of pseudo-liberalism, can have extremely dangerous effects in the realm of politics and social life.

The analysis of individuals and of collective movements shows over and over again that both of these are contaminated with their polar opposites — that the collectivist may be a secret pleromatic mystic and the pleromatic a secret nihilist. This contamination, which may be understood in terms of the unconscious tendency to compensation, reinforces the instability of its victims and makes them, despite their apparent dogmatic certainty, an easy prey to counter-infection of any kind.

Owing to their condition of inner splitness, dogmatically one-sided individuals form an exceedingly insecure intermediate class, which breaks down, and always must break down, in any situation which involves genuine conflict and decision. The textbook example of such a breakdown is provided by the bourgeois class, which is numbered among the representatives of the old ethic, and (in Germany, for example) has a marked strain of pleromatic idealism in its outlook. The breakdown of this class — a phenomenon by no means confined to Germany, as the future will show — has always been an enigma. Their strong ethical will at the conscious level seemed to qualify the representatives of this class to be independent moral individuals and protagonists of the old ethic; unconsciously, however, they were in fact to a large extent in the grip of the opposite side, which they had repressed. One-sided individuals and groups of this type are by nature members of the fifth column, without being aware of the fact; actually they belong to the enemy camp of their own conscious ideology, because in them the shadow is more dynamically alive than the moral ego of the conscious system. In the hour of decision, people of this kind make a complete volte-face and go over to the enemy camp. The pacts which they so often conclude with the enemy forces have their deepest motivation in their own real condition of inner splitness.

The instability of attitude which is caused by the presence of the counter-position in the unconscious is not confined to the average man, who, as a constituent member of the mass, makes up the following of all "movements"; it is also found — and this is even more dangerous — among so-called leading personalities such as educationists, teachers and politicians.

The incompetence of the politicians, which has become so cruelly and sanguinarily obvious to modern man, is essentially due to their human inadequacy — that is, to a moral undermining of their psychic structure which culminates in their total breakdown when faced with any real decision. To future ages, the fact that the leading politicians of our period were not required to pass a test of any kind to determine their human and moral qualifications will appear exactly as grotesque as it would seem to us today if a diphtheria-carrier were to be placed in charge of the children's ward in a hospital.

From the point of view of the new ethic, the moral inadequacy of a politician does not reside in the fact that on the conscious level he is not a morally acceptable personality — though there is no guarantee that he will be that, either! It is his total unconsciousness of the shadow and the illusory orientation of consciousness that accompanies this kind of unawareness which is the decisive — and, often enough, the fatally decisive — factor.

The only person who is morally acceptable in the eyes of the new ethic is the person who has accepted his shadow problem — the person, that is to say, who has become conscious of his own negative side. The danger which constantly threatens the human race and which has dominated history up to the present time arises out of the "untestedness" of leaders who may actually be men of integrity as understood by the old ethic, but whose unconscious and unheeded counter-reactions have generally made more "history" than their conscious attitudes. It is precisely because we realise today that the unconscious is often, if not always, a more powerful determinant in the life of a man than his conscious attitude, his will and his intentions, that we can no longer pretend to be satisfied with a so-called "positive outlook" which is no more than a symptom of the conscious mind. Naturally, this process must not be reversed – and in fact it may well seem axiomatic that acceptance of the shadow cannot be brought about by identification with it. And yet, as the history of the breakthrough of the dark side in the West has taught us, reversals of the old ethic such as those exemplified by the devil-worshipping cults of the Middle Ages can occur and have actually made world history.

The new ethic rejects the hegemony of a partial structure of the personality, and postulates the total personality as the basis of ethical conduct. An ethic which is based on the shadow is just as one-sided as one that is guided solely by ego-values. It leads to suppression, blockage and the breakthrough of compensatory positive forces; but the instability of man's psychic structure is just as marked in an ethic of this kind as it was in the case of the old ethic. A negative, terroristic ethic of dictatorship, force and an opportunism which denies the dignity of the human individual is just as much a partial ethic as was its Judaeo-Christian predecessor. The result is the same in either case, the only difference being that the part of the scapegoat has now to be played by what the old ethic regarded as positive values.

The new ethic is "total" in the sense that it is orientated towards wholeness – and towards two aspects of wholeness in particular. In the first place, it is no longer individualistic; it does not merely take into account the ethical situation of the individual, but also considers the effect which the individual's attitude will have upon the collective. In the second place, it is no longer a partial ethic of consciousness, but also includes within its reckoning the effect of the conscious attitude upon the unconscious. In fact, responsibility now has to be carried by the totality of the personality, not simply by the ego as the centre of consciousness.

These two widenings of our ethical horizon are intimately connected. From the point of view of the external collective, the attention which now has to be paid to the shadow includes primitive mass man in the scope of ethical responsibility; at the same time, from the point of view of the individual as seen from within, this corresponds to a responsible relationship with the primitive mass man who exists as an inner component in every personality.

The external collective with its archaic tendencies has its internal representative in the collective unconscious of each individual. The archaic tendencies and images of the collective unconscious which symbolise the world of instinct are the precipitate of the collective ancestral experience of man; they show us, in fact, the typical way in which he has always reacted and experienced life. But this same collective unconscious also rules the masses and finds its precipitate and expression in the mass phenomena of the external collective.

The new ethic was born under the ruling star of the fuller insight, deeper truth and clearer-sighted awareness of human nature as a whole which is the real achievement of depth psychology. From this point of view, the moral problem of the individual is constellated in the first place by the coexistence of ego and shadow, and the responsibility of the personality is extended so as to include the unconscious or at any rate the personal component of the unconscious, that part of it which contains the figure of the shadow.

Responsibility for the group presupposes a personality which has become conscious of its shadow problem, and which has come to grips with this problem with all the forces at its disposal. The individual must work through his own basic moral problem before he is in a position to play a responsible part in the collective. The realisation of one's own imperfection which is involved in the acceptance of the shadow is a hard task in which the individual is required to free himself from the absolutism of his pleromatic fixation as well as from his identification with collective values.

The "reduction" of the personality which is brought about by the acceptance of the shadow is only apparent. What is actually reduced is an illusory identification of the ego with the absolute – that is to say, an unreal and partial idealisation of the personality which is in any case torpedoed by its polar opposite – the reality and influence of the unconscious. The sacrifice of the absolute ideal of perfection which was taught by the old partial ethic most certainly does not lead to any kind of diminution in the value of humanity. The elimination of the negative effects of the splitting processes would in itself represent such an enormous gain in terms of actual human living that the new ethical demand for the acceptance of the negative would be justified by this alone.

It is for this reason that the accusation that the new ethic is derived from "the urge to make one's own life easier"[1] falls to the ground; equally false is the charge of opportunism and love of comfort, as contrasted with the radicalism and rigour of the old ethic. This ethical rigorousness never in fact extended beyond a partial ethic of consciousness; the very idea of an attempt to apply it to the total personality was unheard of. The dangers of rigorism, on the other hand, are enormous. Again and again in the course of history we find that the disastrous influence of criminal personalities is matched by that of only one other class of people – the radical idealists, dogmatists and absolutists. Nero and Cesare Borgia are in fact only rivalled by Torquemada and Robespierre.

The new ethic is based on an attempt to become conscious of both the positive and the negative forces in the human organism and to relate these forces consciously to the life of the individual and the community. The shadow who demands

[1] Karl Jaspers, *Man in the Modern Age.*

94

acceptance is the outcast of life. He is the individual form which the dark side of humanity takes on in me and for me, as a component of my own personality.

My own shadow side is a part and a representative of the shadow side of the whole human race; and if my shadow is anti-social and greedy, cruel and malicious, poor and miserable – if he approaches me in the form of a beggar, a negro or a wild beast – then my reconciliation with him will involve at the same time my reconciliation with the dark brother of the whole human race. This means that when I accept him and, in him, myself, I am also accepting, in his person, that whole component of the human race which – as my shadow – is "my neighbour".

Here the love of one's neighbour preached by Jesus of Nazareth becomes love of one's neighbour in the form of the thief[1] and the shadow. When restricted to a figure within the personality, this appears to be a paradoxical form of "self-love", in contrast to the unselfish love preached by the Nazarene. Psychologically, however, love and acceptance of the shadow is the essential basis for the actual achievement of an ethical attitude towards the "Thou" who is outside me.

In the psychology of the scapegoat, the denial of the negative (and with it, that self-justification which is such a characteristic feature) leads directly to a denial of the love of one's neighbour. In contrast to the primitive Christian ethic of Jesus of Nazareth himself, the Christian ethic as we know it has never been successful in transcending this dichotomy; on principle, it has always held fast to a Gnostic dualistic conception of an upper and a lower man, a duality between this and the other world, both in man himself and in the universe.

It is only when I have experienced myself as dark (not as a sinner) that I shall be successful in accepting the dark ego in my neighbour; I realise my solidarity with him precisely because "I too am dark", *not* simply because "I too am light".

[1] There is a reference here to the penitent "thief" on the Cross – (*Trans.*).

The self-experience involved in the journey of depth psychology (the first stage of which is the encounter with the shadow) makes man poorer in illusions but richer in insight and understanding; the enlargement of the personality brought about by contact with the shadow opens up a new channel of communication, not only with one's own inner depths but also with the dark side of the human race as a whole. The acceptance of the shadow involves a growth in depth into the ground of one's own being, and with the loss of the airy illusion of an ego-ideal, a new depth and rootedness and stability is born.

This living relationship with the shadow brings home to the ego its solidarity with the whole human species and its history as known in subjective experience, since it discovers within itself a host of prehistoric psychic structures in the form of drives, instincts, primeval images, symbols, archetypal ideas and primitive behaviour patterns.

This encounter makes us conscious of man's group psychology, and at the same time of the fundamental fact that the realm of the ego and of the conscious mind which differentiates people from each other only occupies a very small part of the whole vast universe of the psyche. That which is specifically human and individual only constitutes the topmost layer of the collective unconscious, which extends right down to the animal level. The efforts made by the conscious ego to cut itself adrift from this common foundation and to identify itself with so-called absolute values which are independent of earthly restrictions are therefore foolish and illusory.

The emergence of pagan elements and symbols in association with the shadow side (but by no means only in that context) is clear evidence of the historical connection which unites us with an earlier human psychic stratum underlying the Judaeo-Christian ethical and religious culture of modern man.

When the ego realises its solidarity with the evil "ugliest man", the predatory man and the ape man in terror in the jungle,[1] its stature is increased by the accession of a most vital factor, the lack of which has precipitated modern man into his present disastrous state of splitness and ego-isolation – and that is, a living relationship with nature and the earth.

But it is not our purpose here to discuss the positive and constructive elements in this deep layer of the unconscious, the elements which assist the growth of consciousness – though these are certainly of crucial importance for the future of the human race. Our sole concern is the encounter with that reality which – from the ego's point of view – is known as Evil.

Surprisingly enough, the analysis of individuals also reveals that the encounter and reconciliation with the shadow is in very many cases a *sine qua non* for the birth of a genuinely tolerant attitude towards other people, other groups and other forms and levels of culture.

We have in fact first to assimilate the primitive side of our own nature before we can arrive at a stable feeling of human solidarity and co-responsibility with the collective. Since the total ethic includes the shadow within the sphere of moral responsibility, it follows that the projection of this component will cease, and together with it the psychology of the scapegoat and the campaign of annihilation waged under the pretext of morality against evil in the person of one's neighbour; its place will be taken by a new approach no longer conditioned by the dubious penal and expiatory attitude of the old ethic.

The acceptance of the shadow is a part of that process of development in which – as we have said – a personality structure is created that unites the systems of the conscious mind and the unconscious. This enlargement of the personality is brought about in the first place by the assimilation and raising to consciousness of certain germinal unconscious contents which direct the conscious mind into new paths, and, secondly, by the

[1] To avoid misunderstanding, it should be noted that what we have here is a psychic image which appears in this form and is projected. The image corresponds to a psychological, not a zoological or anthropological fact.

incorporation and transformation of "negative" unconscious contents — that is to say, contents which appear to be hostile to the ego and the conscious mind.

We have learned from the experience of depth psychology that these contents are autonomous. The unconscious is made up of an abundance of unintegrated partial contents with separate tendencies of their own (the complexes discovered by Jung). These lead a split-off but exceedingly real and effective life of their own in the unconscious, beyond the control of ego-consciousness.

The life of both pathological and normal individuals and (to an even greater extent) the life of social groups is conditioned by the hidden effect of these autonomous unconscious contents. Apart from negative contents such as the shadow, a positive unconscious content such as, for example, an instinct or arche-type can work its will in the life of an individual with a power all its own, while the ego remains completely unaware of the influence to which it is exposed.

The instability of a group or individual varies directly with the extent of the area occupied by unconscious contents and inversely with the scope of consciousness. This law is as valid in normal psychology as it is in the psychopathology of the individual or group. An example is the exceptionally high level of instability among primitives or in masses of people, where the influence of affect is notoriously strong.

Since, however, as we have repeatedly stressed, primitive and mass psychology are to be found deep-rooted in each individual, this law can be verified everywhere and in everyone. The instability, unpredictability and unaccountability of a given person increase in inverse ratio to the level of his con-sciousness and directly with the degree of activation of the zone of the autonomous unconscious contents. Apart from certain basic constitutional crises of development such as childhood or puberty, an activation of this kind can also occur (without conscious intention) in sickness, sleep or certain states of poisoning or intoxication; it can be consciously induced for religious or cultic purposes; or, alternatively, it can be brought about by some mass influence which recollectivises the individual and reduces him to the level of a primitive man.

In all these and similar situations the result is a disintegration of the personality. This means that the unity of the personality, which is normally represented by the ego, is dissolved, and a partial content of the unconscious, a complex – an activated instinctual constellation, for example – takes command and works its will independently of those trends in the conscious mind which had been recognised by the ego as guide-lines in the previous situation.

As an illustration of this kind of reduction of the personality, we have cited the case of inundation by the shadow, in which the rejected and repressed contents once more simply have their way.

To fulfil its function, the new ethic will have to make use of quite different methods, tendencies and attitudes than the old. The tension between the opposites which, in the form of dualism, was the distinguishing mark of the old ethic, can by no means be simply abolished and denied.

If, instead of suppressing and repressing the contents of the unconscious, the new ethic is to "accept" them and articulate them with the conscious mind, it will inevitably be faced with the task of their assimilation.

The incorporation of these contents into a greater totality, which is not the given totality of consciousness as it used to be, is the work of the process of individuation. In this process, contents which were previously split-off and autonomous are joined up to form parts of a comprehensive psychic structure which is connected with the ego and the conscious mind, and so receive a different meaning and value in the hierarchy.

Our purpose in this study is only to describe the basic principles and contents of the new ethic, not to illustrate these by means of case material. A detailed account of the transformation

99

of a negative unconscious content into a content of the conscious mind and of the way in which this alteration is brought about has been given elsewhere.[1]

[1] Cf. C. G. Jung, *Psychology and Religion*, C.W.11; C. G. Jung, *The Integration of the Personality*, (Routledge and Kegan Paul) London, 1952; C. G. Jung, *Psychology and Alchemy*, C.W.12.

CHAPTER V

THE AIMS AND VALUES OF THE NEW ETHIC

The main function of the new ethic is to bring about a process of integration, and its first aim is to make the dissociated components, which are hostile to the individual's programme for living, capable of integration. The juxtaposition of opposites which makes up the totality of the world of experience can no longer be resolved by the victory of one side and the repression of the other, but only a synthesis of these opposites.

The ultimate aspiration of the old ethic was partition, differentiation and dichotomy, as formulated in the mythological projection of the Last Judgement under the image of the separation of the sheep from the goats, the good from the evil; the ideal of the new ethic, on the other hand, is the combination of the opposites in a unitary structure. Out of the multitude of conflicting forces, the plurality of the opposites, a structure has to be built which will combine these opposing forces, and in which the manifold diversity of the pairs of the opposites will be held together in the firm embrace of a supra-ordinated unity. The value of the structure which is finally achieved will be proportionate to the strength of the tension between the combined opposites and the number of the polar forces which enter into the new combination.[1]

[1] The structure of wholeness which is achieved by the integration of the psychic components is the fulfilment of a basic tendency in the personality—centroversion—the development of which we have described

The aim of the new ethic is the achievement of wholeness, of the totality of the personality. In this wholeness, the inherent contrast between the two systems of the conscious mind and the unconscious does not fall apart into a condition of splitness, and the purposive directedness of ego-consciousness is not undermined by the opposite tendencies of unconscious contents of which the ego and the conscious mind are entirely unaware. In the new ethical situation, ego-consciousness becomes the locus of responsibility for a psychological League of Nations, to which various groups of states belong, primitive and pre-human as well as differentiated and modern, and in which atheistic and religious, instinctive and spiritual, destructive and constructive elements are represented in varying degrees and coexist with each other.

All these groups of forces must be taken into consideration, since here, as in the collective life of nations, suppression or repression leads to hostile reactions which disturb the life of the whole community and keep it in a state of continual unrest.

The principal requirement of the new ethic is not that the individual should be "good", but that he should be psychologically autonomous — that is to say, healthy and productive, and yet at the same time not psychologically infectious. And the autonomy of the ethical personality means essentially that the assimilation and use of the negative forces to be found in every psychic system takes place as far as possible consciously, within the process of self-realisation. In fact, the central happening in the process of individuation is precisely the way in which the ego takes part in this transformation of the personality, by acting, suffering, shaping and being overwhelmed at the same time. Under the old ethic, it was a frequent, if not a regular, occurrence that a strong "ethical" personality did not live out

---

elsewhere. Centroversion, which arises out of the principle of wholeness in the personality, and which aims at the achievement and maintenance of this wholeness, is made conscious by the ego and taken over in the activity of the total ethic.

his own negative drives, but projected them forcibly on to the weak spots in the environment, so that the negative suppressed and repressed contents had to work themselves out by compensation in his immediate surroundings (the family or the collective), without the "repressor" personality having the slightest notion of his moral responsibility for these phenomena.

The ethical aim of being "non-infectious" may appear to have a purely negative content. This negative limitation, however, is compensated by the principle of wholeness in the personality, the effects of which extend far beyond ethics and the problem of evil, which is our concern here. The wholeness of the personality and its autonomy and integrity as understood by the new ethic actually form the basis for creative processes which give birth to new values. It is these processes which supply the real evidence that the personality has in fact achieved a structure of wholeness and that the work of re-centring has been successful. But to be non-infectious is, if anything, almost more important than to be creative. It is true that the collective does depend on the creative achievement of the individual; yet it can better afford to dispense with creativity than allow itself to become exposed to the unconscious contagious influence of unintegrated and, in that sense, psychologically unhealthy persons.

In the final analysis, it is once again the psychology of the scapegoat which provides us with a general category that also includes this type of infection of one's immediate personal environment. It is a fact (though it cannot be documented here) that, owing to the primary unconscious identity of groups, the transmission and reception of psychological contents to and from the environment is both possible and of frequent occurrence. Numerous examples of this can be quoted from the psychology of children and primitives.[1]

Ethical autonomy and an ethic of wholeness require that each

[1] Cf. Frances Wickes, *The Inner World of Childhood*, New York, 1966; L. Lévy-Bruhl, op. cit., etc.

one of us should, himself, consciously undertake the management of his own shadow. Freud is entirely right when he says, "There is really no such thing as the extermination of evil";[1] since, however, this statement also relates to the individual, it is the duty of each personality to live and suffer the evil which falls to its lot in a spirit of freely accepted responsibility.

When evil works unconsciously and emits its radio-activity underground, it possesses the deadly efficiency of an epidemic; on the other hand, evil done consciously by the ego and accepted as its own personal responsibility does not infect the environment, but is encountered by the ego as its own problem and as a content to be incorporated into life and the integration of the personality like any other psychic content[2].

"Dealing with" a content is the popular expression for what we know as integration. Accepting, dealing with, digesting, working through, growing beyond – all these are formulations for this process of assimilation. They describe various stages in the effort made by the personality to make itself master of a new content – alien and often hostile to the ego though this may be – without, however, defending itself, as the old ethic did, by the use of suppression and repression.

We have shown elsewhere how the development of the ego and of consciousness in the individual follows the archetypal pattern laid down by the life and exploits of the mythical hero. One of the basic conflicts in the life of the hero and, therefore, in the development of every personality arises out of the doing of evil. "Separation of the world parents" and "murder of the primal parents" – these are the great symbols that describe the deed and crime of the hero, which is, however, at the same time the essential act for the liberation of the ego. So, too, in the normal life of the individual, the symbolic murder of the parents or its equivalent is a phase of development which cannot

[1] Sigmund Freud, *For the Times on War and Death.*
[2] C. G. Jung, "After the Catastrophe", C.W.10; *see also* note on pp. 130–31.

be omitted with impunity; often enough, as a large number of cases of retarded development have taught us, the advantage of being a "good child", who shrinks from the "murder" of his parents, is purchased at the perilous cost of the sacrifice of one's independence in later life.

The psychological analysis of any normal development will make it clear that, if he is to grow up, it is not merely unavoidable but actually essential that the individual should do and assimilate a certain amount of evil, and that he should be able to overcome the conflicts involved in this process. The achievement of independence involves the capacity of the ego not only to adopt the values of the collective but often also to secure the fulfilment of those needs of the individual which run counter to collective values – and this entails doing evil.

In the psychological development of the individual, we are again and again confronted by the problem that the "Voice", in contradistinction to conscience, demands that what appears to the ego to be "evil" should be done, and that the inner and outer conflict which arises out of this situation should be accepted, with all its difficulties. Surprisingly often, the avoidance of evil and of the conflict which evil brings in its train turns out to be "unethical" from the standpoint of the "Voice".

In normal cultural periods, when the personality is contained within the cultural canon, and is able to recognise its value as genuine, the emotional vitality of man's deeper layers also finds adequate expression.[1] Religion and art, ritual and custom are so completely saturated with symbolism that the normal life of the individual – even if not of the "Great Individual" – is contained in a living way within the culture of its time.

In periods of violent change, on the other hand – periods marked by the decline of a cultural canon – the individual falls out of this condition of containedness, and into the hands of the primeval powers and gods, whether for life or for death. This

[1] Cf. the author's op. cit., Part II.

105

means, in terms of the real life situation of the individual, that he is exposed to the dangers of direct experience, unprotected by the bulwark of any kind of convention. For example, this problem may appear in the form of a conflict in relationship, in which conventional morality is confronted by the onset of a passionate love. Anyone who fails to take this problem seriously will find himself in a situation of the greatest peril. It is no longer possible for the individual to retain his balance simply by clinging to the traditional law; the result of this may be disturbances and distortions in development which ancient man — and in fact any mythological view of the world which knows the transpersonal powers as gods — would have interpreted as "Aphrodite's revenge".

The peril of a divine invasion is the peril of a living experience of the deep layer in the psyche whose numinous power and suprapersonal claims cannot be shut out — unless indeed we are to shut out vitality, depth and the suprapersonal dimension at the same time — to our own ruin. It is at this point that the conflict arises: we have to do what is "evil" from the point of view of the cultural canon — not indeed in any irresponsible spirit, by allowing ourselves unconsciously to be carried away, but by consciously enduring the conflict involved in the "acceptance of evil" which the "intervention of the Godhead" demands in this case.

From the point of view of the old ethic, the evasion of this conflict and of the suffering which it entails is laudable and good, even at the cost of the risk that the happening which is "avoided" in reality may be lived out in fantasy. That a man's "morally legitimate" human relationship may be poisoned in this way, and that not only he himself but his entire personal environment may fall a victim to this kind of infection is often enough only discovered by the analytical probing of his situation made necessary by the disturbances which appear in the train of his moral "victory".

Disturbances of this type which may arise in outside reality are, however, no more than one, and by no means the only, aspect of this problem. Responsibility for the totality of the personality, which is demanded by the total ethic, is not confined to external reality but also covers the inner reality of dreams, fantasies, thoughts, etc. This reality of the psyche obliges us to recognise that a fantasy can have effects just as serious as those of an act – a truth which has long been taught in the Far East. The decisive part played by psychic reality – as depth psychology is just beginning to discover – is a more powerful influence behind the scenes than the naive consciousness of average Western man has ever dreamt of. Individuals and groups – and nations, too, and movements in history – are conditioned by the power of inner psychic realities which often enough appear in the first place as fantasies in the mind of an individual. This influence of the inner world is to be found at work in such diverse spheres as politics and religion, technology and art. War and destruction are repeatedly let loose to devastate the world at the behest of men driven by fantasies of power; at the same time, the inner images of creative artists become the cultural possession of the whole human race.

Yet the reality of the inner world also implies that the acceptance of evil does not, in every case and for every person, involve *external* action. Often enough, what is required is the exact opposite of realising an inner image in the concrete language of outer reality. But to realise it and to live it from within is by no means the same as simply to abreact it. The multiplicity and complexity of this situation makes any kind of theoretical prescription for ethical conduct completely impossible. External and internal constellation, psychological and constitutional type, age and individual make-up – such are the vital components of every ethical decision; and every ethical decision will for this reason present a different appearance, since one man's good can be another man's evil – and vice versa.

Moral judgement must in principle be restricted in this way, since it is impossible to predict the psychological form in which evil will appear in the life story of any given individual. At the same time, the experience of depth psychology and the crisis confronting modern man (and in particular his inability to live within the categories of the old ethic) make it necessary to arrive at formulations which will have at least approximate general validity. This means that the "demands" of the new ethic must be regarded as in a certain sense only "formal"; their realisation *in concreto* must be left to the unique and fateful processes by which every individual has to fight his way through to his own decisions.

And yet, though it is true that the "demands" of the new ethic can only be realised in individual terms, it is no less true that the moral situation of modern man remains, in spite of all personal variations, essentially a general problem. The crystallised precipitate left behind by the recurrence of certain typical patterns in a multitude of individual lives can in fact be formulated in general terms.

"Making good", as understood by the old ethic, with the attendant repression of evil and obedience to convention, is often enough no more than an easy way out, which shirks peril and clings to established security. Yet "where peril lies, grows the remedy too", and the voice of the new ethic, or so it seems, is determined to accept both peril and remedy at the same time — since the one is not to be had without the other.

This in itself makes it perfectly clear that the way of the new ethic is anything rather than a "way of making one's own life easier". Quite the contrary. To surrender the moral certainty about good and evil provided by the old ethic, stamped as it was with the approval of the collective, and to accept the ambiguity of the inner experience is always a difficult undertaking for the individual, since in every case it involves a venture into the unknown, with all the danger which the acceptance of evil brings with it for every responsible ego.

This situation is graphically exemplified by the following dream of a Jewish woman from Israel.

"I am with X in Jaffa. Suddenly, there is a crowd, I am separated from X and find myself alone and surrounded by Arabs. An Arab grins and seizes hold of me, but many others rush up to him, tear him away from me, and shout abuse and curses at him. 'She is reserved for the King!' they cry. New situation. I am standing on a bridge; there is no-one present except Arabs; I know that escape is impossible. I also know that I am to marry the son of the Arab King. I reflect for a moment. I am very sad at being parted from X. But nothing can be done about it now. I think, 'There is no way out, so it's really better if I give my consent.' A priest standing near me says, 'We can only redeem those that become impure.' 'Of course,' I think, 'one must first become impure, that is, dare to do something, before one can be redeemed.' The priest then says, 'Osiris is also to be found below'."

One or two points need to be made in connection with the interpretation of this dream. In particular, it is necessary to forestall the misunderstanding that the acceptance of evil has to be acted out externally and is the result of a negative, unsatisfactory situation. The woman in our dream, for example, had a sexually and emotionally happy relationship with X and was in no sense "unsatisfied".

For Jews in Israel, Jaffa and Arabs are very often shadow symbols with a sexual colouring. But it is clear from the sacral symbolism of the dream that the basic situation of "becoming impure" is not restricted to the sexual sphere. Both the reservation of the dreamer for the "King" and the mention of the Egyptian Osiris, king and god of the dead and of resurrection point to the deeper and higher meaning of this happening.

The "acceptance of evil" is therefore in this case enacted essentially in the inner realm, as a process of transformation of the personality. The sacral sexual symbolism of the fantasies which break through in this dream are to be understood, as not infrequently happens, in the spirit of Goethe's "hallowed longing" – that is to say, as a "spiritual marriage" such as is pre-figured in the myth by the relationship between Isis and the dead Osiris.[1]

However, this is not the place for a detailed interpretation of the meaning of this dream. We simply wish to consider here the connection between "becoming impure" and "redemption". It is actually the purity of her conscious outlook and her determination to cling to this which has to be surrendered by this woman – not for the sake of a higher purity, but in order that she may experience the transformation promised her by Osiris and the underworld – a transformation which will in fact bring her into relationship with darkness and with the abyss.

What has to be sacrificed in this context is innocence and unambiguous certitude. It was only by experiencing "impurity" as the element which she lacked that this woman was able to realise herself, and to arrive at a new philosophy and appraisal of life which is no longer simply collective and conventional, but which has its roots in a state of redemption in which light and darkness, purity and impurity are alike contained.

The courage to make an individual appraisal of values which declares its independence of the values of the collective in matters of good and evil is one of the most difficult demands made on the individual by the new ethic. In most cases this results in a severe psychic conflict; the values of the collective possess their own inner representative in the shape of the individual's super-ego. Acceptance of the Voice does not involve indiscriminate approval of everything which comes from inside – any more than acceptance of the negative side involves acting out the negative without any resistance.

What *is* implied by the fulfilment of the new ethical demand is that the share of evil "allotted" to an individual by his constitution or personal fate should be worked through and deliberately endured by him. In the process, to an extent which varies with the individual, part of the negative side must be consciously lived. And it is no small part of the task of depth

[1] Cf. the author's op. cit., Part I.

110

psychology to enable the individual to become capable of living in this world by acquiring the moral courage not to want to be either worse *or better* than he actually is.

It is, in fact, generally people whose ethical standards are over-exalted who find the acceptance of the negative in practice such a burning problem. A person of this kind had the following dream.

"There is a heap of letters in front of me which have to be rubbed clean. After I have finished some of them, a large hand scoops into the heap and is going to take them all away. I want to call out, 'But the letters are not nearly all finished yet!'

"I am standing in front of a large book. Many of the letters are dark and dingy, but I am given to understand that I could find a way of seeing that they, too, in reality glitter and shine. They have a shining side, but it is hidden."

We do not need to know the dreamer's association with the Cabala and the exoteric and esoteric teaching in order to realise that the reference here is to the holy and secret knowledge of the light side of darkness. But one has to find a way of learning to recognise this basic fact of existence – and one has to be a person who "wanted to rub all the letters clean" – that is, "who ever strives with might and main" to do good as understood by the old ethic.[1]

Those who exploit the acceptance of evil as a means of making life easy for themselves are invariably people of a primitive type who have yet to experience the values of the old ethic. It is not necessary for such people to acquire the technique of repression, but they do need to cultivate the capacity for suppression and sacrifice, discipline and asceticism, since without this they will never achieve the ego-stability required by civilised man in the first place.

Once again, we are confronted here with the hierarchical principle in the new ethic, which implies that this ethic cannot

[1] Quoted from Goethe's *Faust*: "Who ever strives with might and main – that is the man we can redeem" – (*Trans.*).

be codified and made the basis of a general law "without respect of persons". The variety of types in the human species and the fact that people living in the same epoch may belong to the most diverse cultural levels and stages of consciousness are among the basic insights of the new ethic.

This range of variation in personality and consciousness is reflected in varying levels of ethical maturity. Where personality development is rudimentary (e.g. where the ego is primitive or infantile), the conventional collective ethic ("the Law") will be adequate; in the case of higher types of personality, on the other hand, in whom wholeness has unfolded its flower, the authority of the "Voice" will replace the collective law of conscience.

In earlier times, this phenomenon only occurred or was observable in ethical geniuses; today, however, it is already affecting far wider circles in the individualised population of the West. It is a symptom of this development that, in the course of the past hundred years, legislation itself has become increasingly discriminating in the account it takes of the individual and of the degree to which he may justly be held responsible in the light of constitutional and psychological factors.

The rejection of the penal principle by the new ethic belongs to the same context. The tendency of punishment is always towards the extermination, suppression and repression of the negative. The object of the technique is not to bring about a transformation of the personality as a whole, but only a "partial-ethical" change — whether real or illusory — in the conscious mind.

It is for this reason that the new ethic, based as it is on depth psychology, is not interested in punishment. It can logically agree, for example, to the elimination of elements which the collective is unable to assimilate, but it does this not on the grounds of the penal principle or of the principle of its own alleged moral superiority, but in the consciousness of its own psychological and biological incapacity. The fact that a given organism cannot digest something is not an argument against the indigestible element as such, but only against the capacity of the organism to assimilate it.

Incipient attempts to put the new ethic into practice can already be seen on every hand – for example, in the liberalisation of the old prison system, in psycho-analytical theories of education, in welfare work on behalf of criminals and in the acceptance of psychological insights by the criminal law. Developments tending in the same direction but starting out from the most disparate ideologies are appearing quite independently of each other – a fact which only confirms our hypothesis that a far-reaching general shift is taking place in the psychic structure of modern man – a shift involving the decline of the old, and the emergence of a new, ethic.

It is required of us that we should "work through" our own evil in an independent and responsible way. But the corollary of this is that becoming conscious must now rank as an ethical duty. The central significance of this demand, in which European man's thirst for scientific knowledge coincides with the new ethic, comes home to us when we realise what havoc can be wrought in both individual and collective by unconsciousness, through its instrument, repression. It is appalling to watch human beings (whether individuals or whole nations) being hollowed out from inside and devoured by the lie which is concealed in repression and in its fatal unwillingness to look reality in the face.

It may actually appear as if the principle of deception has taken the place occupied by evil in the old ethic, and as if all that has happened in the new ethic is a change in the content of what is regarded as evil. But the real point at issue is quite different. The principle of truth in the new ethic is bound up with the authenticity of the relationship between the ego and the unconscious. The ethical duty of awareness implies that consciousness is called in as an authority to create and control the relationship to wholeness of everything psychic – the relationship, that is, between the contents of the unconscious and the conscious mind. This task does not depend on the nature of the content which is to be brought into relationship with consciousness or on whether that content is good or evil as understood by the old ethic. The decisive factor from the ethical point of view is now the criterion of truth. In this context, the fact and the extent of self-awareness emerges as a value in the ethical, not in the scientific sense of that term.

The acknowledgement of one's own evil is "good". To be too good — that is, to want to transcend the limits of the good which is actually available and possible — is "evil". Evil done by anybody in a conscious way (and that always also implies full awareness of his own responsibility), evil, in fact, from which the agent does not try to escape — is ethically "good". The repression of evil, accompanied, as it invariably is, by an inflationary overvaluation of oneself, is "evil", even when it is the result of a "positive attitude" or a "good will".

At first sight, the close relationship between the new ethic and awareness and the stress which this lays on the conscious mind and the ego may appear excessively rationalistic, and insufficient justice may seem to be done to the instinctive — that is, unconscious — way in which a human person as a totality may be capable of living with his own evil. Later on, however, we shall see that, in spite of the stress now laid upon it, the ego does not possess the ultimate power of decision in the new ethic.

The conscious doing of evil stands in direct contrast to what is described as "sublimation" in the Freudian meaning of that term. Sublimation is regarded as a trick, by means of which evil is "denaturalised" and then applied to a cultural purpose. But this sublimation of Freud's is an example of unconscious adaptation, and should not be understood as a conscious direction of libido. When a "blood-thirsty" person, whose nature contains an excess of aggressive instinctive components, becomes a butcher, a soldier or a surgeon, we have an example of a type of "sublimation" in which the primitive urge to shed blood is incorporated into forms of satisfaction which are more or less conducive to culture and sanctioned by the community. We cannot deal with the obscure subject of sublimation and the problem of its occurrence in this context; the following remarks must suffice.

Sublimation can occur in cases where a "pre-disposition towards the transformation of egotistical into social drives"[1] in the form of an "inherited behaviour pattern" is already present. Where this kind of structure exists, however, there is no ethical problem. On the other hand, experience shows that sublimation which is willed (that is, directed by the ego and the conscious mind) is only possible to a very limited extent; in effect, the ego cannot divert natural instinctive tendencies to cultural ends.

Where such a possibility does exist, however, we are caught in the vicious circle of the old ethic; very frequently, sublimation of this type is purchased at the cost of the contagious miasma which arises out of the repression and suppression of the unconscious elements which are not susceptible to sublimation. We know those sublimating saints, whose "unspotted" lives (as understood by the old ethic) are free from lived-out sexuality and full of brotherly love – on the conscious level, at any rate. But our sharpened insight cannot fail to notice the hellish aureole which so often emanates from "holiness" of this kind. On the periphery of its radiantly pure centre, we detect its counterpart – the corona of perverse sexual fantasies which "the Devil" sends as a temptation, and the ring of blood and fire in which the unbelievers are persecuted – all the inhuman cruelty, in fact, the burnings, tortures, pogroms and crusades which give the lie to the brotherly love and the "sublimations" of the conscious mind.

This type of holiness has become loathsome in our eyes, in whatever form it may manifest itself – whether it appears as the holiness of the inquisitor or of the party boss – for we have

[1] Sigmund Freud, "For the Times on War and Death".

learned that all these things are one and the same phenomenon, and that the differences are only differences of costume and period, not of degrees of humanity or its opposite.

The old ethical position of "absolute obligation" has, as its necessary corollary, the doctrine of "original sin" – which represents the impossibility of fulfilling the absolute obligation. The logical consequence of this situation was the rejection of "life in this world", the rejection of earth and the earthly, and, not least, the rejection of man himself. Life, earth and man were denied, as the carriers of evil and of the negative. In all the various manifestations of the flight from life – in the ego-devaluation of an overwhelming sense of sin just as much as in the ego-inflation of self-sanctification – man was really escaping from this "under" side of the world, away into heaven as the symbol of the positive and good.

In contrast to this, the new ethic, with its acceptance of the negative, represents both the self-affirmation of modern man and his acceptance of the earth and of life in this world. Characteristically enough, the new orientation always appears under the sign of the Descent into Hell – and even of the pact with the Devil.

The alliance between Faust and Mephisto is the alliance of modern man with the shadow and with evil, which makes it possible for him in the first place to undertake his journey through the fullness of life, right down to the Mothers and up again to the Eternal Feminine. This journey does not by-pass guilt, but leads through the *entire* world of the living, and it is no accident that it penetrates deep downwards into the pagan stratum of reality underlying the Judaic and the Christian layers. In the period after Faust, the figure of Pan emerges again and again from the unconscious of modern man – the prototype of the Christian Devil, complete and unabridged – and Pan, in his capacity as the custodian of the secrets of Nature, brings with him the key to the depths. This time, the tempter is not refused but accepted, for it seems that, nowadays, it is only the man who, as he "strives with might and main", does not shun the danger of downfall and of chaos, that "can be redeemed".

By accepting evil, modern man accepts the world and himself in the dangerous double nature which belongs to them both. This self-affirmation is to be understood in the deepest sense as an affirmation of our human totality, which embraces the unconscious as well as the conscious mind, and whose centre is not the ego (which is only the centre of consciousness), nor yet the so-called super-ego, but the Self. This Self is a limit-concept for the conscious mind – that is to say, the conscious mind cannot apprehend it rationally. But it is possible to say something about its emergence and the form in which it appears.

Before we illustrate the idea of the Self by comparing it with the super-ego, a simple analogy may help to clarify the nature of this concept. When we consider the multiplicity of the transactions which occur in the human body and the incredibly complex hierarchies of interrelationships between the biochemical and the neuro-psychological processes involved (of which only separate partial systems can ever be fully comprehended by science), we are still perfectly well aware that this same body also functions in a unitary way as a single organism possessing a totality. All the various partial systems, from the ultra-microscopic processes (whether perceptible or invisible) in the individual cell to major systems such as the circulation of the blood or the reactions of the nervous system, work together in a co-ordinated fashion and are attuned to each other in a symphony of mutual interdependence.

These processes together constitute a unity, the virtual centre of which is the Self or entelechy, which is a symbol for the phenomenon of the totality of the organism. The total structure in its capacity as a super-ordinate factor above all these partial interrelationships can also be conceived of as a centre, which directs and controls them as its circumference. This control of all partial processes from an invisible centre is the most obvious phenomenon which differentiates the living from the inorganic.[1]

The scientific investigation of causal relationships has nothing to do with this indispensable teleological way of looking at the organism. The Self as the centre of all things psychic, which also includes within itself the processes of the unconscious, is at the same time identical with the totality of the body, since, as we have to assume, and to some extent can already demonstrate, all psychic processes have, at the least, their physical correlates.

This is not the place to discuss the problem – so vital to the psychology of the neuroses – of the relationship between the body and the psyche. We must, however, draw attention to the fact that inclusion of the unconscious always entails inclusion of the body at the same time. When we speak of the earth, then this "earth" is symbolically identical with the body – just as flight from the earth is always at the same time flight from the body. But the totality of the body, in its unitariness and centredness, works unconsciously as a natural phenomenon in everything organic. What distinguishes the human situation, on the other hand, is the fact that in the psychic realm the tension between the opposites of conscious and unconscious has developed in the course of history and has culminated in a separation of the opposites as a whole. This separation between the opposites, the poles of which can be formulated in terms of conscious/ unconscious, spirit/life, above/below, heaven/earth or in other symbols of a mythological, philosophical, moral or religious character, is, in itself, indispensable to the development of consciousness; it has, however, been exacerbated to a point where it has proved disastrous for both the individual and the collective. In fact, the opposites have been torn asunder so violently that man himself has got lost in the tension between them. As a result, man's whole position in the world – and not only that, but the whole process which enables human beings to live together in societies – is now very gravely jeopardised.

[1] Cf. the concept of centroversion in Neumann, op. cit.

At first sight, the developmental tendency towards whole-ness appears to be no more than an individual requirement; it emerges as such among the individual processes of development in the shape of the need, or rather the urgent necessity, to evolve a stable psychic structure which can stand firm against the tendencies towards disintegration in the outside world and in the unconscious.

The whole process of individuation and its significance for the individual is a problem which we cannot deal with in this con-text. Jung has laid bare the anatomy of individuation and illus-trated it with a wealth of pertinent material. But the relevance of this process to ethics is to be found in the fact that the trend towards a stabilisation of the personality is of absolutely crucial significance from the moral point of view.

Here, too, it is possible for us to trace the transition to a new epoch in the development of mankind.

The evolution of law, of a generally binding moral code and of collective values, and the formation and development of conscience and the super-ego served the purpose of building up the ego and the system of the conscious mind and of liberating this system from the original state in which it was overwhelmed by the unconscious. The development of consciousness itself, and everything that has followed in its train, owes its origin to the urgent need for the creation of a stable structure to stand firm against the tendencies towards disintegration in the unconscious and in the outside world. Collective values further the cause of this development, and conscience, the psychological authority which represents collective values in the individual, originally performed the positive function of protecting both individual and collective from relapsing into an emotional state in which they were blindly driven by the unconscious.

In this sense, although it is true to say that the super-ego, with its moral standard derived from outside, represents an alien, heteronomous ethic, it nevertheless stands for a point of view superior to that of the primitive ego and is, at this stage of development, a valid – though relative – incarnation of the Self.

The primitive ego is an infantile ego. It encounters the collective in the shape of the super-ego, equipped with the whole might of external authority. Conscience (felt as "social anxiety"), the law with its principle of rewards and punishments, and the feeling of guilt *vis-à-vis* the cultural super-ego are – so far as we are aware – the primary moral experience for the infantile ego of early man. The relationship between the infantile individual ego and the collective super-ego is regularly portrayed by the image of the relationship between father and child. But this fact of symbology by no means justifies the derivation of morality from the family romance.

The Oedipus complex is a myth, and, as a myth, it is true. However, when it was interpreted by Freud personalistically, in terms of the family romance, cause and effect became inverted. Freud's theory of the primal father is only a thinly disguised version of the old story of Adam and Eve as the origin of the human family. The fact that in Freud the Adam and Eve family has been extended to form the primal horde in no way alters the original position that the family history of Adam and Sons is simply postulated as the origin of human development.

The paradox of the murder of the father, if this is understood in concrete terms, is revealed in a singularly clear light when we realise that we are obliged to assume that the drama of parricide, as depicted by Freud in *Totem and Taboo*, has been enacted in reality on innumerable occasions and must be supposed to have repeated itself universally, if it is to account for the origin of the super-ego.

The existence and crucial importance of the Oedipus complex are not in question at all. That is – and remains – Freud's momentous discovery. It is the confusion of the father-archetype with the personal father which here, as so often, leads to error – a confusion which is suggested by the fact that in childhood the father-archetype is projected on to the personal father.

The father-archetype, however, is a symbol, an image, in which at a certain stage of development, the infantile ego of early man experiences the impact of the collective super-ego. To put it in a graphic but over-simplified way, we could say that the small individual ego experiences the supra-individual collective, to which it owes its origin and which controls its destiny and prescribes its values, in the form of the father-archetype. At any rate, this is the case in all patriarchal cultures. It is precisely the group-identity of early times which makes this experience of the "ego spark" intelligible.

What psycho-analysis reduces and explains away is, in reality, the decisive factor. The fact that the father-archetype as it appears in the totem is understood to be something specifically non-human is a symbolic expression of the real situation. What is being experienced is not something personally known, but a strange supra-personal numinous reality. And that is the way in which primitive man does actually experience the essential otherness of the animal, the most frequent embodiment of the totem.

Where the personal father appears to the infantile ego as the representative of the collective and of collective values (as is generally the case in the patriarchal world), the father-archetype is projected on to him and experienced in him, the personal father. Thus Freud's statement, "What is begun in the father is completed in the mass"[1] requires to be precisely inverted. From the point of view of historical development, the supra-personal collective contents appear both phylogenetically and ontogenically before the formation of the personal contents relating to the ego, and it is only later that the personal sphere, and together with it the development of the ego, crystallises out of the collective background. The myth precedes the family

[1] Freud, *Civilisation and its Discontents*, translated by Joan Riviere, London, 1930.

romance, just as the collective unconscious only relaxes its hold on the ego and the sphere of the conscious mind at a comparatively late period.[1]

Conscience, as the representative of the collective super-ego, is a heteronomous influence which comes from outside, quite irrespective of whether this influence encourages the development of consciousness or not. The external authority of the super-ego, which possesses the character of givenness, stability, fixity and unbending tradition, is opposed by the "Voice", in its capacity as an ordaining and determining factor, the expression of an inner revelation of a new and progressively unfolding development — of that which is to come, in fact.

Always and inevitably, the Voice possesses the character of a "son" *vis-à-vis* the "father" character of the law; and the murder of the father by the son will always remain an eternal primordial image of the inner history of mankind and of individual man. This relationship is by no means peculiar to the son-religion of Christianity and the father-religion of Judaism. The same archetype governs the murder of the Pope-Father (this, of course, is what the Pope really is) by Luther the heretic and, in Judaism (looking at it from the opposite point of view), the son-revolution of Hasidism against the typical paternal position of rabbinism.[2]

The recollectivisation process of modern times, the mass character of which confronts the individual with yet another threat of disintegration, leads, by way of compensation, to a new tendency towards stability in the shape of the process of individuation. This attempt at stabilisation is no longer based on the stability of the conscious mind alone, but on that of a totalised psychic structure.

[1] Cf. the concept of secondary personalisation in Neumann, op. cit.

[2] "Son-character" in this context means the proclamation of the new, in contrast to the old, which possesses "father-character". When the new is raised to the power of the dominant principle, it generally itself assumes "father-character" once again.

The role of the super-ego as the representative of a heterono-mous ethic deriving from outside and super-ordinate to the infantile ego is now taken over by the Self, which appears as the inner centre of the personality. Adult ego-consciousness, which has become independent and lost its infantile character in the course of the process of individualisation in the West, now orientates itself by "itself", or by the Self as the centre of the totality of the psyche.

This installation of the Self to fill the place of the heterono-mous super-ego is an expression of the newly-won ethical autonomy of the personality. The term "installation" is used here of the Self in the same sense in which the phenomenon of the "installation" and proclamation of a god is known to us from the history of religion. In this ritual, the divinity is con-sciously appointed and recognised by the ego as an authoritative control centre. Before that time, though the divinity – like the Self – had certainly performed the function of an authoritative control centre, the ego had not been aware of this fact. This means that the "installation" embodies a change in the situation and experience of the ego, and is not in any sense an act which results in something "happening" to the "Self".

From now on, the ego can no longer perform its duty to the Self by the simple method of orientating itself in the light of the established values; a process of continuous self-questioning and self-control is now required. Admittedly, this is carried out by the ego; we have emphasised the fact that this ethical duty is taken over by the conscious mind. Its aim, however, is not a questioning of conscience in the sense of an examination of the motives and contents of the conscious mind; the scope of the enquiry is now much more the total structure of the personality – and this includes the unconscious.

The basic phenomenon on which the ego is able to rely for this purpose is psychic compensation. This implies that there is a relationship between the unconscious and the conscious mind of such a nature that contents missing from the conscious system and required for totality or wholeness will appear in an accentuated form in the unconscious. The effect of this law of compensation is that, for example, a wrong attitude of the conscious mind will be corrected in a dream by night, or that a principle suppressed in conscious living but vitally important for life as a whole – an instinct or some other content – will demand its share of attention by appearing in the form of a fantasy, a dream, a slip or a disturbance of some kind.

Compensation is a direct expression of wholeness and, therefore, of the Self. It does not concern itself with partial structures such as the conscious mind or the unconscious, in any one-sided way; on the contrary, it is precisely the wholeness of the psyche which is asserting its primacy in this context over the arbitrary deviations of the partial systems.

Analogous examples of direction from the centre of wholeness are to be found, as we have emphasised, throughout the realm of the organic. Co-operation between particular sub-systems is only made possible in the first place by the effect of compensatory homeostatic phenomena. A conscious mind which pays attention to this principle of compensation in the psychic realm, and not only observes its manifestations but also actually reacts to them, therefore represents a genuine orientation of the ego to the Self. In the process of self-questioning, the centre of gravity of the personality is gradually shifted away from the ego and the conscious mind towards the Self and the phenomenon of the wholeness of the psyche.

The logic underlying our contention that the trend of development which relates ethics to the psyche in its capacity as a unitary whole leads to the stability of the personality will now be apparent. The instability which is brought about by the splitting-off of the shadow side, with all its catastrophic results, is avoided if the shadow and the unconscious remain under the control of the conscious mind and the ego is engaged in a constant effort to link them up with consciousness and real life. In this way, the process of integration, with its careful attention to compensatory phenomena and its orientation to the Self and to wholeness, leads to a personality structure which can no longer be disintegrated by the conflict between the opposites and the predominance of one side or the other.

The middle way, along which the development of the personality now proceeds, is free from the one-sidedness of the dogmatic, absolute valuation which was previously imposed on the partial systems. It is free from sheer "goodness" and sheer "evil", and equally free from the one-sidedness alternatives of a purely rationalistic conscious attitude or a fixed ideology of irrationalism. In the process, too, the personality is delivered from the disastrous dialectic under whose sway any given one-sided attitude is repeatedly and violently replaced by its equally one-sided counterposition.

This freedom from the opposites and this "middle way" are by no means to be confused with their illustrious predecessors in the Orient. Our middle way does have certain features in common with its Oriental counterpart, the most notable being ethical autonomy and the partial independence of the world which this confers; in contrast, however, to the hostility to the world which is characteristic of Eastern spirituality, the new way is quite specifically concerned to strengthen and deepen our "being-in-the-world", and it is this which makes possible the process of centring in the Self and the inclusion of the unconscious elements within the structure of the personality. In practice, the assimilation of unconscious components leaves little room for sublimation. Apart from the realisation of negative contents under conscious control, the major and decisive part is played by the *transformation* of such contents within the personality.

The transformation of the negative was the basic psychological problem of alchemy. As Jung has shown[1] the transformation of lead, the basest, into gold, the most precious, metal, was

[1] See Wilhelm and Jung, *The Secret of the Golden Flower*, London and New York, 1931; C. G. Jung, *Psychology and Alchemy*, C.W.12, etc.

understood as a psychic process by the alchemists themselves.

The same problem is found in a parallel but different form in the Cabala and in Hasidism, a movement of religious renewal which gripped the masses in East European Jewry more than a hundred and fifty years ago. Such statements as "The most holy sparks are to be found at the lowest level" and "Goodness is hidden in the dark" refer to this same process of transformation; so, too, does the interpretation of the commandment, "Thou shalt love God with thy whole heart" as meaning "Thou shalt love God with both thy good and thine evil instincts".

The full significance of this conception was only grasped by a few of the leaders of Hasidism, and not by Judaism as a whole. It is most clearly expressed in the following interpretation. In the text, "Thou shalt love thy neighbour as thyself: I am the LORD",[1] the Hebrew word translated by "thy neighbour" is replaced by the word meaning "thine evil", which sounds the same, though it is spelt differently. The text then reads, "Thou shalt love thine evil as thyself: I am the LORD", and the interpretation is as follows: "As thou doest, so do I, the LORD", in other words, "As thou lovest thine evil, so do I love it."[2]

It is not our concern here to describe how the transformation of evil and the negative within the personality takes place. It is a part of the process of individuation, in which, even in modern man, alchemical symbols typically occur; these point to the transformative character of the experience. The transformation, in which the personality suffers a change, by being as it were cooked and smelted, is often also connected with symbols of rebirth and is always essentially a process of "becoming whole".

We arrive, then, at the following formulation of values in the new ethic: whatever leads to wholeness is "good"; whatever leads to splitting is "evil". Integration is good, disintegration is evil. Life, constructive tendencies and integration are on the

[1] Lev. 19:18.
[2] Torat Rabbi Nachmann, p. 73 (S. A. Horodetsky).

side of good; death, splitting and disintegration are on the side of evil. At the same time, however, modern man is aware of the indissoluble interdependence of the two principles. On balance, however, it is a fact that the processes of integration do predominate; this is no less true of the living soul than it is of living matter in general. Our estimate of ethical values is no longer concerned with contents, qualities or actions considered as "entities"; it is related functionally to the whole. Whatever helps that wholeness which is centred on the Self towards integration is "good", irrespective of the nature of this helping factor. And, vice versa, whatever leads to disintegration is "evil" – even if it is "good will", "collectively sanctioned values" or anything else "intrinsically good".

The incorporation of the negative in the process of integration is the criterion not only of power but of ethical achievement. This will remain true even though, often enough, this "achievement" is in effect a kind of suffering and may actually take on the appearance of failure – or express itself in terms of real failure. Suffering, too – the acceptance and assimilation of suffering – is an achievement and an expression of the psychological vitality of the individual. That this is not a matter of our seeking out evil, but of evil, as it were, knocking on our door, scarcely requires further emphasis. As it is assimilated, however, this evil that knocks on our door is built into the wholeness of the personality, without the necessary character of opposition between "good" and "evil" being effaced in the process. The living wholeness in fact lives from the tension between the pairs of opposites which are bound together in it to form a superordinate unity, whether these opposites are good and evil, masculine and feminine, outer and inner, rational and irrational or others.

The wholeness in unity of conscious and unconscious combines in its development both the lower and the higher powers. The danger of splitting has as much to be combated when spiritual, heavenly powers have the upper hand, as when instinctive, earthly forces are predominant. A development which overcomes the one-sidedness of nature, whether this is determined by psychological type or by sex, is the ideal of the new ethic, in which modern man is making a sincere attempt to cease denying the reality of the world in his value judgements, and, instead, to accept the world and to incorporate it into a higher synthesis within himself.

It is for this reason that one of the basic symbols of the process of individuation is the mandala or holy circle. In this symbol, the psyche achieves perfection of form, the configuration, for example, of a sphere or a blossom expressing the roundness of a soul at harmony with itself, in which the quaternity of the psychic functions, the polarity between masculine and feminine and the inherited part-personalities of the unconscious, with all their multitude of opposites, are integrated in a unitary structure.

From one point of view, the new ethic is an individual ethic, an ethic of individuation. It formulates the unique task of each individual (unique since it arises out of the uniqueness of his constellation), which is to grapple with his own specific moral problems as they arise out of his own psycho-physical constitution and destiny. But the other aspect of the new ethic, which is of at least equal importance, is precisely the collective significance of the individuation which it entails. What we spoke of as the stability of the psychic structure is, as we have already emphasised, most vitally relevant to the collective.

We have described the constellation of the old ethic as "contagious" because in this ethic the negative is not accepted by the individual and assimilated, transformed, lived and suffered, but is thrust out and split off from the conscious mind, with the result that it migrates into the primitive sections of the group, where it causes inflammation and outbreaks of disorder.

On the other hand, the personality which has found its centre and achieved its ethical autonomy, as understood by the total ethic, constitutes, with its stabilised structure and enlarged awareness, a rallying point and a bulwark for the collective. It is a focus of stillness amid the flux of phenomena, and the waves of collectivism and of the mass psyche will break against it in vain, whether they attack it from the outside or from within. Those waves in fact only sweep away personalities which have developed along the lines of a partial ethic, since the roots of such personalities are not grounded in the unconscious. They are overwhelmed by the sheer weight of the mass happenings around them and within, which appear in the guise of an alien tyranny, as we can observe on every side in the contemporary scene.

The consolidated psychic structure of the man of the total ethic is not so gravely exposed to danger, for the simple reason that he has assimilated and incorporated a great many elements from the mass psyche, the collective unconscious, which overpower other men with horror, amazement, admiration or compulsive attraction. A personality of this kind is better acquainted with both the heights and the depths and chasms of human nature, since it has experienced and lived them within itself. In the catastrophes of psychic indundation which characterise periods of violent collective upheaval, such a personality forms a breakwater against mass epidemics and the flood of events by which they are accompanied, and acts as a guardian and a purifier of the collective. As C. G. Jung put it, "personality ... does not allow itself to be seized by the panic terror of those who are just waking to consciousness, for it has put all its terrors behind it. It is able to cope with the changing times, and has unknowingly and involuntarily become a *leader*".[1]

This kind of assimilation by an individual of contents active in the collective is known to us, for example, from the Old Testament prophets. They experienced the shadow side of the people and its perils in the first place within themselves, and were then able to proclaim its onslaught in advance of the actual event; conversely, when disaster came, they were the first to

[1] C.W.17, p. 179.

experience in themselves the emergence from the depths of constructive forces and the possibilities of deliverance, and were then able to exteriorise these in the form of consolation and the promise of recovery in the future.

To the extent that he does live in reality the whole range of his particular life, the individual is, as we said at the beginning, an alchemical retort, in which the elements present in the collective are melted down and refashioned to form a new synthesis, which is then offered to the collective. But the pre-digestion of evil which he carries out as part of the process of assimilating his shadow makes him, at the same time, an agent for the immunisation of the collective. An individual's shadow is invariably bound up with the collective shadow of his group, and as he digests his own evil, a fragment of the collective evil is invariably co-digested at the same time.

In contrast to the scapegoat psychology, in which the individual eliminates his own evil by projecting it on to the weaker brethren, we now find that the exact opposite is happening: we encounter the phenomenon of "vicarious suffering". The individual assumes personal responsibility for part of the burden of the collective, and he decontaminates this evil by integrating it into his own inner process of transformation. If the operation is successful, it leads to an inner liberation of the collective, which in part at least is redeemed from this evil.[1]

[1] The ideas expressed in this book (most of which was completed in 1943) are carried a stage further by C. G. Jung's important remarks on the concept of psychological collective guilt in *Essays on Contemporary Events* 1947, p. 46 ff.; C.W.10, p. 194 ff.).

"Psychological" collective guilt is based on the fact that, owing to the unconscious identity of all individual group members — that is to say, owing to their "participation mystique" — the group psyche is, to a large extent, the dominant factor within the collective. It is a corollary of this that the group ethic is responsible for the actions of the collective. In group affairs, individual ethics are suspended — an example being the suspension in war of the taboo on killing which is normally binding on the individual. But this logically implies the collective responsibility of all members of the group for group actions which are carried out under the primitive group

When we encounter the problem of vicarious suffering and redemption, we are already deep inside the territory of religion, which is indissolubly bound up with ethics. Owing to his acceptance of the dark side, the individual is continually reminded of the relativity of his constitution, of the earthbound nature of his existence and of his co-dependence on instincts and drives; in the process, he becomes humanised. So, too, he now encounters the divine itself in a human form – that is to say, he experiences it not in the absoluteness of the abstract or of an infinity without content, but in the relative finitude of a real revelation within the human realm – as a Voice.

It is precisely when the dark side of life is accepted that possibilities of new experience begin to open up – not only in ethics but also in religion. These possibilities run counter, it is true, to the old ethic and the old type of religion associated with it; they have the advantage, however, that they are in a position to combine the vitality of our new image of man with the new and transformed image of God which is emerging.

On the human level, the assimilation of the shadow provides a link between the ego and those layers of the psyche which

---

ethic (see p. 60 above). This is the real basis for "psychological" collective guilt, and it has to be recognised as such by the individual, since he is a member of the group. Another result of moral regression to the group ethic is the introduction of collective punishment. To the consciousness of the "innocent" individual, this seems at first sight to be unjust. But when the part played by the individual as a total person in group affairs is included in the sphere of moral responsibility (in the spirit of the total ethic), then our ethical evaluation will also change. In this sense, the recognition and acceptance of collective guilt is in fact a commandment of the new ethic, since for this ethic the responsibility of man is not confined to his conscious outlook.

The whole question of justice in the relationship between the individual and the collective was already discussed with penetrating clarity in the confrontation between Abraham and Jahweh which took place before the fall of Sodom (Gen. 18: 23 ff.). This discussion, too, in which Abraham protested against the "righteous being slain with the wicked", ended with a recognition of the collective guilt even of the righteous.

correspond to the world of the inferior function and the level of primitive man. Behind the personal moral problems of the individual, the moral problem of the collective to which the individual belongs comes into view, and this involves making conscious his collective mendacities and repressions, his inadequacies and his parochialism in time. The final stage to be revealed, however, is the moral problem of the whole human race, which is at the same time the moral problem of the Godhead.

At this point in our inner experience, the moral problem transcends the limits of the personal and becomes the wider problem of evil in the human race or of evil in itself — that is to say, in theological terms, the problem of evil in God. The new ethic is in agreement with the original conception of Judaism, according to which the Deity created light and darkness, good and evil, and in which God and Satan were not separated from one another, but were interrelated aspects of the numinous. This apparently primitive trait in the Jewish conception of God implies that, side by side with the image of God the Father, God's irrational power aspect was explicitly retained, as a matter of living experience.

In classical Judaism, the man of God was by no means necessarily distinguished by the high level of his ethical conduct. The relationship between the divine and the world in which man was actually incorporated was originally brought about by listening to the inner Voice of the divine in man, not by the performance of prescribed ethical duties. Abraham, who deserted his father, Jacob the deceiver, Moses the man-slaughterer and David the adulterer were by no means crowned with the halo of the victorious subduer of the dragon of darkness — though traits of this kind were also to be found in their nature. In fact, their personalities cast a long shadow, but it was precisely for this reason that the centre of their being remained in contact with the Godhead, in whose image they had been created. For this Godhead was itself not simply all-good and all-wise, but righteousness and grace met wrath and jealousy, the intelligible coexisted with the incomprehensible, and light and darkness were at work together in its unfathomable depths at the self-same time.

In the dream of a modern man, the Voice of someone invisible called out to the dreamer (who was trying to evade spectral presences of disease and death), "God loves his plague, too!" The message and injunction of this sentence shatters the old ethic, shatters with it the old formulation of the problem of the opposites and compels the ego to seek a new orientation, which will demand a relativisation of good and evil as the precondition for a valid life.

"Stop fighting the plague! Stop simply accepting and enduring it — and love it, instead!" Is this, then, to be the paradoxical demand which confronts the man who is seeking an ethical orientation? At once a perilous abyss of madness, crime and death opens, yawning, at our feet. Is there any sense at all in speaking of "orientation" in this context? Is this not rather the negation of all ethics — a senseless and completely unrealisable temptation, in fact, in which what used to be known as Satan but now parades in modern dress as the demands of the unconscious is luring us to our destruction?

It is perfectly true that the element of horror in this proposition transcends all possibilities of human realisation; yet it does contain a self-revelation of the Godhead which puts an end once and for all to the naivety of the traditional ethical conception that rends God's world asunder into light and darkness, pure and impure, healthy and sick. The creator of light and darkness, of the good and of the evil instinct, of health and of sickness, confronts modern man in the unity of his numinous ambivalence with an unfathomable power, in comparison with which the orientation of the old ethic is clearly exposed as an excessively self-assured and infantile standpoint.

The emergence of the new ethic, and of the new ethical demand that man should take responsibility for himself as a total unit, carries the implication that the time has now come for the principle of perfection to be sacrificed on the altar of wholeness. The total ethic corresponds to an actual state of imperfection which embraces man, the world and the Godhead, since the Godhead itself is also imperfect because, and in so far as, it contains within itself the principle of the opposites.

The state of wholeness beyond the opposites which has to be created is a unity in which the demands not only of aesthetics and ethics, but also of religion, coincide. The injunction that we should consciously recognise this unity and work out a new attitude towards this wholeness points the way to one of the basic tasks of modern man. This new human standpoint which accepts darkness and the negative side, combines within itself the positive elements of Christianity, the world affirmation of Judaism and the secular concentration on this earth characteristic of modern man, who has reacted to the collapse of the anthropocentric cosmos with a shift in emphasis towards supra-personal human values and the brotherhood of man which is becoming clearer every day.

The downfall of the old world-orientation and the resultant dethronement of man has led to a chaotic psychological situation. Modern man now sees himself as a peripheral creature on a tiny planet in a physically dead infinity, relativised by a knowledge of his own conditioned and preconditioned existence and restricted in his opportunities for redemption by the limits imposed by human nature in general and by his own individual psycho-physical constitution in particular.

Our growing insight into the limitations of the human condition must inevitably lead, in the course of the next few centuries, to an increasing sense of human solidarity and to a recognition of the fact that, despite all differences, the structure of human nature is everywhere, in essence, the same. The common rootedness of all religion and philosophy in the collective unconscious of the human race is beginning to become obvious. It is becoming clear that, although different archetypal constellations may be dominant or recessive among different nations and races and at different times, the human species is nevertheless one and indivisible in the basic structure of its mind.

But just as this solidarity of our species accounts for the inner history of mankind, so the unity of the planet earth will determine the history of the future. It is as though mankind, gripped as it is by the icy cold of empty, lifeless, cosmic space, which stares at it horribly from every side, sans God, sans soul and sans humanity, has no other option than to huddle closer together, if it is to hold its own against this tyrant power. Slowly but surely, the human race is withdrawing the psychological projections by means of which it had peopled the emptiness of the world with hierarchies of gods and spirits, heavens and hells; and now, with amazement, for the first time, it is experiencing the creative fullness of its own primal psychic Ground.

And yet, out of the midst of this circle of humanity, which is beginning to take shape from the coming-together of every part of the human species — nations and races, continents and cultures — the same creative Godhead, unformed and manifold, is emerging within the human mind, who previously filled the heavens and spheres of the universe around us.

REFLECTIONS ON THE SHADOW

At first sight, it may appear that the shadow is no more than a problem of secondary interest and importance, since it is generally regarded as a figure belonging to the personal unconscious — that is to say, to the uppermost layer of those deep unconscious processes which analytical psychology has selected as its special field of study. The object of this paper, however, is to establish that the problem of the shadow is a *central* concern of modern psychology as such, and that the range of subjects which it involves are among the profoundest questions which analytical psychology has attempted to answer. It is not our purpose to recapitulate here what Jung has said about the shadow in many passages in his writings;[2] it must suffice to recall that the shadow is the unknown side of the personality, and that it normally encounters the ego, the centre and representative of the light side and of consciousness, in the form of a dark, uncanny figure of evil — to confront whom is always a fateful experience for the individual.

[1] This Appendix originally appeared as an article in *Der Psychologe* Vol. II *Heft* 7/8 July/August 1950. (This was a special number published on the occasion of Jung's seventy-fifth birthday.) It had been the author's intention to add this article to a second edition of the book in order to clarify the concept of the shadow.

[2] See especially *Psychological Types*; *The Relations between the Ego and the Unconscious*, C.W.7; *Archetypes and the Collective Unconscious*, C.W.9 Part I; *Psychology and Religion*, C.W.11; *A Psychological Approach to the Dogma of the Trinity*, C.W.11; and *Aion*, C.W.9 Part II, Ch. II.

In mythology, the figures of the hostile brothers (for example, Osiris – Set, Balder – Loki, Abel – Cain, Jacob – Esau), the antagonists such as Siegfried and Hagen, Faust and Mephisto, Dr. Jekyll and Mr. Hyde, and the "Doppelgänger" figures of fairy tale and poetry[1] are projections of that interdependence between opposites which links the ego with the shadow. The appearance of these figures in mythology is evidence in itself that what is presented here for our discussion is a universal human problem which completely transcends any purely personal problems of the individual.

At first, the figure of the shadow is experienced externally as an alien and an enemy, but in the course of its progressive realisation in consciousness it is introjected and recognised as a component of one's own personality. Yet when the personal shadow has been assimilated, the *archetypal shadow* (in the form of the Devil or Adversary) still remains potent in the psyche. This archetypal shadow-figure has a specific meaning for man as his antagonist in the process of development towards consciousness. The same insight – that the psychological basis for the phenomenon of the shadow is to be found in man's development towards consciousness – was formulated by Jung in the following terms.

"The enlargement of the light side of consciousness has the necessary consequence that that part of the psyche which is less light and less capable of consciousness is thrown into darkness to such an extent that sooner or later a rift occurs in the psychic system. At first, this is not recognised as such and is therefore projected – i.e. it appears as a religious projection, in the form of a split between the powers of Light and Darkness."[2]

This "rift", which in a more or less obvious form runs through the psyche of every modern person, occurs when the processes of differentiation which lead to the development of consciousness endanger the means of communication with the

[1] Cf. Hoffman, Chamisso, Edgar Allan Poe, etc.
[2] Jung, *The Symbolism of the Spirit: The Spirit Mercurius*, C.W.13.

dark side of the unconscious.[1] Man learns to identify himself as far as possible with the ego as the centre of the conscious mind; he learns to comply with the ethical demands presented to him by the collective and to identify himself to a large extent with the light world of moral values and of consciousness, and at the same time to do his best to rid himself of the so-called "anti-values" by the techniques of suppression and repression.[2]

Evidence of this "rift" in the psychic system is to be found in the fact that the split personality identifies itself with the powers of light, but leaves the powers of darkness (the shadow side) in projected form and then experiences and combats them in the shape of "the evil out there". This scapegoat psychology not only produces the most disastrous effects on the life of the collective (where it leads to wars and the extermination of groups holding minority opinions); it also gravely endangers the individual. It endangers him no less when he appears to have succeeded in ridding himself of his dark side than when he fails and is threatened or overwhelmed by the "powers of darkness". The condition of being threatened and overwhelmed by the dark element, which breaks through from the "other side", beyond the rift, is exemplified by the mental breakdowns with which modern depth psychology is so frequently confronted nowadays. The fact that these breakdowns are brought about by "the unconscious" means of course that it is the "dark side" which — for good or for ill — is asserting its claim to consideration. This implies that the mental sickness of modern man is largely due to his own condition of inner splitness; and to act as if the powers of darkness do not belong to his own psyche is no kind of solution to the problem. Man has to realise that he possesses a shadow which is the dark side of his own personality; he is being compelled to recognise his "inferior function",[3] if only for the reason that he is so often overwhelmed by it, with the result

[1] See the author's *The Origins and History of Consciousness*, Pt. II.
[2] Cf. pp. 34–35 of the present volume.
[3] See Jung, *Psychological Types*, C.W.6.

that the light world of his conscious mind and his ethical values succumbs to an invasion by the dark side. The whole suffering brought upon man by his experience of the inherent evil in his own nature—the whole immeasurable problem of "original sin", in fact—threatens to annihilate the individual in a welter of anxiety and feelings of guilt.

It is precisely when the problem of the shadow has reached this critical point that a decisive new development occurs—a development which has made Jung's analytical psychology the bearer of a new consciousness of humanity for modern man. Freud still regarded sexuality pessimistically, from a reductive point of view, as a power from the dark side of the unconscious which would have to be "sublimated"; in his opinion, the assimilation of the unconscious led, at best, to "Civilization and its Discontents". Jung stands in direct contrast to this viewpoint. In spite of his unrivalled knowledge of the perils of the deep layer of the human psyche, he has a great and revolutionary faith in the creativity of human nature, and it is precisely the dark and ambiguous figure of the shadow which—according to analytical psychology—holds the key to a positive development that may be destined to lead the way to a new wholeness in modern man and to heal the disastrous "rift" in humanity.

Under the old order, the excessive demands made on human nature in the name of the Absolute and of its slogan "*Omne bonum a deo, omne malum ab homine*"[1] had led to a disastrous widening of the gulf between light and darkness in the psyche, and had left man with only two alternatives—either to be overwhelmed by his consciousness of the shadow, to acknowledge himself to be a sinner, and then to be "saved" by the intervention of religion—or else to make a radical attempt to rid himself of the dark side altogether. It is at this point that Jung appears as the healer of modern man and, in a truly superb and revolutionary counter-movement, places himself on the side of

[1] "All good comes from God, all evil from man"; see Jung *Aion*, C.W.9 Pt. II, p. 46.

humanity, on the side of the creature – and on the side of the shadow.

"This 'inferior' personality is made up of everything that will not fit in with, and adapt to, the laws and regulations of conscious life. It is compounded of 'disobedience' and is therefore rejected not on moral grounds only, but also for reasons of expediency . . . But this integration (of the inferior function) cannot take place and be put to a useful purpose unless one can admit the tendencies bound up with the shadow and allow them some measure of realization – tempered, of course, with the necessary criticism. This leads to disobedience and self-disgust, but also to self-reliance, without which individuation is unthinkable. The ability to 'will otherwise' must, unfortunately, be real if ethics are to make any sense at all."[1]

This disobedience, however, is not to be understood in terms of disobedience to society: its meaning is rather existential and primary – it is one of the basic structural components which make up the total human situation.

"Through the intervention of the Holy Ghost, however, man is included in the divine process, and this means that the principle of separateness and autonomy over against God – which is personified in Lucifer as the God-opposing will – is included in it too. But for this will there would have been no creation and no work of salvation either. The shadow and the opposing will are the necessary conditions for all actualization. An object that has no will of its own, capable, if need be, of opposing its creator, and with no qualities other than its creator's, such an object has no independent existence and is incapable of ethical decision . . . Therefore Lucifer was perhaps the one who best understood the divine will struggling to create a world and who carried out that will most faithfully. For, by rebelling against God, he became the active principle of a creation which opposed to God a counter-will of its own."[2]

[1] Jung, *A Psychological Approach to the Dogma of the Trinity*, C.W.11, p. 198.
[2] Ibid, p. 196.

141

The acceptance of man's shadow side does not only result in succour and healing; it includes an element of forgiveness and absolution. Man learns more than simply to live on tolerable terms with himself; he must actually learn to live with his sin — though this, of course, must not be misunderstood as meaning to live "in" his sin. This brings us to the heart of the moral and psychological problem which the realisation of the shadow involves for human development, and which, in Jung's words, "should not be twisted into an intellectual activity, for it has far more the meaning of a suffering and a passion which implicate the whole man".[1]

In every case, the acceptance of the shadow is preceded by a mortal conflict, in which the ego struggles to the last to defend its own world of values; it is only through suffering that it finally arrives at an awareness of a new ethic, in which the ego and the conscious mind are no longer responsible for the sole and ultimate decision. At first, for both patient and therapist, the shadow is Evil — and Evil is that which is to be avoided.

"But we assiduously avoid investigating whether in this very power of evil God might have placed some special purpose which it is most important for us to know. One often feels driven to some such view when, like the psychotherapist, one has to deal with people who are confronted with their blackest shadow. At any rate, the doctor cannot afford to point, with a gesture of facile moral superiority, to the tablets of the law and say, 'Thou shalt not'. He has to examine things objectively and weigh up possibilities, for he knows, less from religious training and education than from instinct and experience, that there is something very like a *felix culpa*.[2] He knows that one can miss not only one's

---

[1] Jung, *The Spirit of Psychology*, C.W.8, p. 208.

[2] "Happy fault", said of Adam's sin. From the Roman Missal, Holy Saturday Rite. The full text runs: "*O felix culpa, quae talem ac tantum meruit habere redemptorem!*" ("O happy fault, which merited so great and glorious a redeemer!") — (*Trans.*).

happiness but also one's final guilt, without which a man will never reach his wholeness."[1]

The acceptance of the problem of the shadow is the first part of a process of transformation in the personality which, whatever else it may include, always involves an enlargement of consciousness. This does not, however, by any means imply an irresponsible surrender to the shadow, which would result in a fatal loss of consciousness. The change of attitude towards the shadow which is essential for the healing of the sick person, who is the representative of modern man in all his splitness and disintegration, has nothing in common with any megalomaniac condition of being "beyond good and evil". On the contrary, the acceptance of oneself as including a dark aspect and a shadow actually springs from a deep and humble recognition of the invincible creatureliness of man, which is a part of the purpose of his creation. Unlike the old unconscious dilemma — either surrender to the shadow and be overwhelmed, or else project it and lose it altogether — "acceptance of the shadow" is a solution which brings unconsciousness of the problem to an end. And that is in fact the point of the process.

"One of the toughest roots of all evil is unconsciousness, and I could wish that the saying of Jesus, 'Man, if thou knowest what thou doest, thou art blessed, but if thou knowest not, thou art accursed, and a transgressor of the law'[2] were still in the gospels, even though it has only one authentic source. It might well be the motto for a new morality."[3]

The shadow is the "guardian of the threshold", across which the path leads into the nether realm of transformation and renewal. And so what first appears to the ego as a devil becomes a psychopomp, a guide of the soul, who leads the way into the underworld of the unconscious — which however includes hell as

[1] Jung, *Psychology and Alchemy*, C.W.12, pp. 29–30.
[2] See James, *The Apocryphal New Testament*, p. 33.
[3] Jung, *A Psychological Approach to the Dogma of the Trinity*, C.W.11, p. 197.

well as the realm of the Mothers. Here too Faust's compact with Mephisto turns out to be the prototype.

Modern man has lost his way; but the road which brings salvation to him is a road which leads downwards to a reunion with the unconscious, with the instinctual world of nature and with the ancestors, whose messenger is the shadow. He it is who brings the "good news" of the treasure hidden in the depths, of the herb of healing which grows in the darkness and whose secret power is able to staunch the Amfortas-wound of modern man.

However, the answer of Jung's analytical psychology to the problem of the shadow is more than simply another example of that "earthing" of modern man which we meet in so many fields today. Depth psychology is, it is true, one of those intellectual currents through which mankind is becoming aware of its kinship with the "lower" levels of reality — as is happening, for example, in ethnology, the science of man as a primitive, in biology, the science of man as a child of nature, and in sociology, the science of man as a creature of the herd. Common to all these different currents is a certain similarity of direction which is typical of the contemporary *Zeitgeist*; on the other hand, depth psychology was born out of the extremity of human need to a far greater degree than any other science.

Depth psychology — and this, of course, includes the analytical psychology of Jung — did not arise out of any preformed conception of man. It is "field work", in which both the therapist, as he makes his desperate attempt to save the individual from his deadly peril, and the sick person himself are constantly surprised and overwhelmed to find that the unpredictable happens, and that meaning and inner guidance suddenly emerge out of what seems pathological and absurd. One of these unpredictable insights is the discovery that, against all expectation, Lucifer, the bringer of Light, chooses the shadow in which to reveal himself. At first, modern man experiences the powers of "evil" as dark forces devoid of all meaning which shatter the world of human consciousness and culture; what he fails to recognise, however, is the origin of these forces within himself. It is only when he is compelled by sickness and extremity to come to terms with his own nature that the opportunity may arise for him gradually to experience this sombre power of the shadow as a messenger from the creative potential which lives in his own psyche. It is part of the destiny of modern man that his way should first lead him "down to the depths", not "up to the heights"; is it then surprising that the guide who meets him as he sets out on his journey should turn out to be no shining angel of light but the dark shadow-figure of his own evil?

It is at this stage, however, that the dark and paradoxical secret of the transformation of the personality begins to become a living experience for him. Even in the actual process of transformation, when the archetypes, the impersonal figures of the collective unconscious, take over the role of guide, and the personal shadow-figure has already, as far as possible, been brought into relationship with the conscious life of the personality, the shadow still exerts its unfathomable power.

This aspect of the process of transformation has been brought out very clearly by Jung in his researches into alchemy. The problem of the shadow is crucial in this context. This is not simply due to the fact that Mercury,[1] the "Spirit" of alchemy, also possesses the attributes of the Devil, and that death, blackness, decomposition and guilt are essential prerequisites of the *opus*, which have to be affirmed and suffered. As Jung has shown, the real, secret, heretical aim of alchemy is not simply to "endure" the shadow and accept him in a passive way but actively to seek him out and to redeem him in the *opus magnum*. It is always the dark and chthonic aspect of the shadow in the nature of man and of the world which is redeemed by the procreation, making or birth of the *filius philosophorum*.[2] It is no

[1] Jung, *The Spirit Mercurius*, C.W.13, pp. 228-9.
[2] Son of the philosophers — (*Trans.*).

accident that the gold is to be found not "in a heavenly place",[1] but *"in stercore"*, in the dung.

The truth is that the process of transformation is bound up with the shadow throughout its course, not just at the beginning of the journey – a secret which is already betrayed by the constant occurrence of the symbol of incest, considered as a sinful action. The creative grace of renewal, healing and transformation, which emerges unexpectedly from the darkness of the unconscious, retains to the last its connection with the paradox of the *deus absconditus*,[2] that unaccountable and inscrutably numinous power which may encounter the human ego under the guise of the Devil, the shadow of God, in the very citadel of the psyche. The Godhead, which infinitely transcends the range of human understanding, is reflected in its own image – the paradox of the human Self. In passage after passage, Jung has been at pains to demonstrate how and why the fourth person, the Devil, the antichrist belongs to the totality of the divine nature and may no longer be excluded from it. It is, however, a complete misunderstanding of the urgency of his deep concern to misinterpret this as theology. His aim is, in every case, "to relate so-called metaphysical concepts, which have lost their root connection with natural experience, to living, universal psychic processes, so that they can recover their true and original meaning".[3]

The mortal peril which confronts modern man is that he may be collectivised by the pressure of mass events, become the plaything of the forces of the unconscious, and finally himself perish in the disintegration of his own consciousness. The analytical psychology of Jung counters this peril by teaching the principle of growth towards wholeness through the process of individuation. But this growth towards wholeness necessarily involves a creative relationship between the dark instinctual

---

[1] ἐν οὐρανίῳ τόπῳ, Plato, *Republic* – (*Trans.*).

[2] Hidden god – (*Trans.*).

[3] Jung, *Aion*, C.W.9, Pt. II, p. 34.

side of man's nature and the light side represented by the conscious mind. A new form of humanism is needed, in which man will learn to make friends with himself and to experience his own shadow side as an essential component of his creative vitality. The shadow is not a transitional stage or "nothing but" the instinctual side considered simply as the soil in which the roots of life are bedded. It is the paradoxical secret of transformation itself, since it is in fact in and through the shadow that the lead is transformed into gold. It is only when man learns to experience himself as the creature of a creator who made light and darkness, good and evil, that he becomes aware of his own Self as a paradoxical totality in which the opposites are linked together as they are in the Godhead. Only then — when the creative interrelationship of light and shadow is accepted and lived as the foundation of this world — is life in this world truly possible for man; only then will the unity of creation and of human existence escape destruction by that disastrous rift which threatens the future of the human race.

INDEX

INDEX

Borgia, Cesare, 94
bourgeois (class and epoch),
  41, 90

Cabala, 111, 126
Cain, 40, 138
canon of values; *see* values
capitalism, 56
Catholicism, 39
centro-version, 101 *n.*, 102 *n.*
Chamisso, A. von, 138 *n.*
China (Chinese), 52, 61
Christ, 28; *see also* Jesus
Christian ethic, 16; *see also*
  Judaeo-Christian ethic
Christian man, 82, 83
Christian Science, 87
Christianity, 84, 122, 134
Codex Bezae, 15
collective, 8, 14, 25, 29–32, 35
  passim 43, 47–8, 50 *passim*
  59, 61 *passim* 70, 72 *passim*
  76, 78 *passim* 90, 92, 93, 94,
  105 *passim* 113, 118 *passim*
  121, 128 *passim* 139, 146
Communism, 52
Community of Individuals, 19
compensation (ethical), 49,
  56, 74, 75, 103, 122–4
conscience, 8, 11, 35–7, 39,
  40–1, 49, 55, 58, 65, 66, 67,
  112, 120, 122
conscious (consciousness), 13,
  15, 17, 22, 25, 26, 28, 35
  passim 147
creative (individual), 19–20,

22, 29–30, 61, 65, 67, 103,
  135, 140, 143, 145, 146–7
criminals, 39, 70, 83, 94, 113
culture—categories, 29, 70,
  105; purposes, 55, 57, 114,
  115; super ego, 120

Dark side (of human personality), 8, 28, 38, 40, 47, 64,
  74, 81, 82 *et seq.*, 92, 95, 96,
  131, 137, 139, 140, 142,
  145, 146, 147
Darwin, Charles, 83
David, 20, 132
deflation (devaluation) of the
  ego, 46, 64, 85, 86, 116
dehumanisation, 44
demiurge, 18
denial (of the negative or
  shadow), 22, 33, 34, 44, 55,
  58, 95
Depth Psychology, 11, 26, 29,
  35, 76, 77 *et seq.*, 84, 93, 96,
  98, 108, 110–11, 139, 144
Descent into Hell, 116
deus absconditus, 146
Devil, 45, 115, 116, 138, 145,
  146; *see also* Lucifer, Satan
dichotomy, 44–5, 95, 101; *see
  also* dualism
discipline, 34, 56, 68, 111
disintegration, 59, 83 *et seq.*,
  88, 119, 126, 127, 143, 146
Doppelgänger figures, 40, 138
Dostoievsky, F. M., 83
dualism, 44–5, 47, 95, 101

Edom, 40
ego-consciousness, 12, 18, 34 *et seq.*, 63–6, 76 *et seq.*, 81–2, 84, *et seq.*, 89, 98, 102, 104, 112, 115, 123
ego-deflation; *see* deflation
ego-inflation, 41–4, 46–7, 79, 80, 84, 85, 87, 116
ego-isolation, 97
ego-stability, 111, 124; *see also* super ego
Elders of Zion, 56
Élite, the, 44, 46, 62–5, 67, 68–73, 89
empiricism, 11, 83
Enlightenment, Period of, 71
epidemics (mass-movements), 27, 50–1, 52 *et seq.*, 57, 69, 74, 90, 91, 104, 129
equality of man, 71–2
Esau, 138
eschatology, 14, 87
ethics; *see* New Ethic, Old Ethic
ethnology, 52, 144
Europe, 12, 25; European man, 113
existentialist dilemma, 44; existentialist insecurity, 84

Façade Personality, 37–9, 53, 68
fanaticism, 28, 42, 88
fantasies, 106–7, 109, 115, 124
Far East, 107; *see also* China, Orient

Fascist, 39, 52
father-archetype, 120–2
Founder-Individual, 62, 64
Frazer, J. G., 50 *n.*
Freud, Sigmund, 35, 37, 54, 77, 79, 81, 83, 114, 115 *n.*, 120

Galileo, Galilei, 55
gentleman, ideal of, 33, 34
Germany, 19, 90; *see also* National Socialism
ghost, man as a disembodied, 43
Gnosticism, 18, 45, 87, 95
God (Godhead), 18, 45, 46, 62, 73, 74, 87, 106, 126, 131, 132–5, 141, 146, 147
Goethe, J. W. von, 30, 109, 111 *n.*
Goliath, 20
Good, the concept of, 11, 15, 27, 33, 47, 114, 125, 127
Gostynin, 23
grace, 46, 133, 146
Great Individual, 61–3, 105
Greek contribution to ethics, 33
group ethic, 60–1, 63 *et seq.*, 80, 93, 96–8
guilt, 26, 50 *et seq.*, 58, 142–6

Hagen, 40, 138
Hasidism (Hasidic Story), 23–4, 122, 126
heresy, 36, 39, 52, 67, 122, 145

sin, 31, 46–7, 51–2, 54, 66, 76, 78, 116, 142; *see also* Original Sin

sociology, 26, 84, 86, 144

Socrates, 39, 55

son-character, 122 *n.*

Spitteler, 35

split-personality, 8, 45, 49, 56, 58, 69, 71, 73–4, 85, 126–7, 143; *see also* disintegration

Stevenson, R. L., 40

sublimation, 114–15, 125, 140

suffering, 34, 44, 47, 50, 54, 102, 106, 127, 130, 140, 142, 145; *see also* vicarious suffering

suicide, 60

super-ego, 36, 37, 110, 117, 119–23

suppression, 8, 34–5, 37, 42, 44, 47–8, 49–50, 58, 66, 68, 69, 74, 103, 111, 112, 115

symbol (symbolism), 15, 29, 33, 34, 43, 45, 93, 96, 104, 105, 117, 118, 120, 126, 128

Technology, 25, 118

Terror (French Reign of), 12

"That art thou" doctrine, 79

Torquemada, 94

totality (ethical), 8–9, 31, 77, 92 *et seq.*, 101 *et seq.*, 117 *et seq.*, 128–9, 134–5, 146–7

tragedy, classical, 64–5; marital, 31

transformation, 58, 77, 99–100, 102, 109–10, 112, 125 *et seq.*, 143–7

transpersonal, 41, 43, 44, 46, 106

ugliest man (Nietzsche's conception of), 40, 82, 96

unconscious, the, 12, 14, 15, 17–18, 28, 29 *passim* 146

utilitarianism, 89

validity (ethical), 13–14, 16, 27, 31, 34, 51

values, canon of, 36, 70, 84

values (collective of Old Ethic), 8–9, 12, 16–17, 27, 29, 31, 35 *passim* 58, 59, 61 *et seq.*, 71, 83 *et seq.*, 110, 112

values (individual) of New Ethic, 103 *et seq.*, 110, 119, 127, 139

vicarious sacrifice, 51, 54

vicarious suffering, 130–1

victims (of shadow projection), 52–4, 59

Victorian age, 71

Vischer, Friedrich Theodor, 14

Voice (inner), 8, 9, 35, 39, 62–3, 67, 73, 105, 110, 122, 131, 133

War, 19, 21, 25, 42, 50, 53, 55, 57–8, 71, 74, 107, 139

West (Western man), 23, 28, 29, 33, 34, 41, 63, 82, 84, 86, 107, 112
wholeness; *see* totality
Wickes, Frances, 103 *n.*
women, problem of, 30

World War I, 42
World War II, 19

Yahweh, 28
yogi, 16

Zeitgeist, 144

CPSIA information can be obtained
at www.ICGtesting.com
Printed in the USA
LVOW11s0241151216
517365LV00001B/56/P